BEFORE
YOU
CLIMB
ANY
HIGHER

JONATHAN McREYNOLDS

BEFORE YOU CLIMB ANY HIGHER

VALLEY WISDOM for MOUNTAIN DREAMS

W PUBLISHING GROUP

AN IMPRINT OF THOMAS NELSON

ISBN 978-1-4003-3889-4 (audiobook)
ISBN 978-1-4003-3888-7 (ePub)
ISBN 978-1-4003-3887-0 (TP)

Library of Congress Control Number: 2024946275

Printed in the United States of America
24 25 26 27 28 LBC 5 4 3 2 1

CONTENTS

THE OPENER

One morning in July, at about seven thirty, a bumpy entrance into a San Antonio parking lot jarred me awake. Lying diagonally on my RV's Murphy bed, I tried to lull myself back into some much-needed rest.

"I'm here with the tour. I have an artist with me," I heard my driver and childhood friend, Junior, announcing to the arena's tunnel-visioned staff. "I'll need shore power."

I sat up and peeked through the divider just enough to see a tough, blank-faced blonde in a neon-yellow polo shirt shake her head in doubt and retort, "Ahh, I don't know about that. Which artist again?"

Junior sighed, not only because he'd been driving all night, but because he had done this dance countless mornings before and could tell exactly where it was going.

"Jonathan McReynolds."

"That's an opener? Ahhh . . . OK," the lady responded.

I have to admit, it's never fun to hear your name *not* move the needle in a situation. So, as she stared blankly at her clipboard, I rolled back over and tried to fall asleep again, hoping that Junior would eventually negotiate, charm, or get lucky, and I'd wake up parked in the shade or next to a power source for my air conditioner. Some cities provided us shade. Some provided electricity. Some gave us both. But some offered neither. Therefore, from city to city, my motorhome was either a state-of-the-art oasis in the hot summer heat or an unpleasant sauna, burning fuel just to keep the temperature under eighty degrees.

Either way, typically by about 7:34 a.m., I would be reminded that I was *just* the opening act.

I gave up on trying to sleep in the steadily warming cabin around eight o'clock that morning and began my daily routine. I made and folded up the Murphy bed, lifted the couch back into its place, and waited—for a sound check that never came.

My road manager was likely somewhere in the arena, fighting for a cooled dressing room, but I had lost my fight for this tour. I relegated myself to my sauna on wheels and tried to work out a few musical ideas in my head.

Fortunately, I had an album to finish, so I could make use of those lonely hours. I picked up and put down my mic, guitar, and laptop at least twenty times over the course of the day, trying to catch a groove. I finally found that groove at about six thirty that evening, just twenty minutes before my name would be annouced. So, I saved my progress and threw on one of my ten stylist-approved outfits, snaked my in-ear monitors down my shirt, and braved the hot Texas evening.

It was cooler *outside* than it was inside the RV.

My roadie guided me through the back of an arena I'd never been inside of, to the side of the stage. I did a little dance to get the blood flowing, took the mic from the stage-hand, and braved a boomy room of thousands. I nodded to my bandmates for the first time all day and hummed to myself just to make sure my voice still worked.

Then, I rocked out.

In the most holy of ways, of course.

And what happened that balmy day in San Antonio happened thirty-six times that summer.

In all, I witnessed three or four hundred thousand people—from Miami to Seattle, from liberal metropolis to flag-waving secondary market—jumping on beat and screaming the choruses.

As if they'd forgotten I was *just* the opener.

That night—as I did every night—I cruised through my set, rarely missing a beat. I played to the fans who already knew my music, then turned my energy toward converting the white girl yawning in her seat.

Unite.

Lead worship.

Sing.

Be impressive.

Be funny.

Be transparent.

Guitar solo.

Piano.

High note.

New song.

Party.

Wave goodbye to ten thousand smiles.

Ignore the few hundred flat faces that wished my bus had run out of gas on the way.

Evade the fragile egos of the other artists and their gofers backstage and make a beeline for my muggy RV again.

Protect my fragile ego.

As soon as the door shut, I took a beat, changed into more comfortable clothes, and opened my laptop. As the headliner's intro blasted through the subwoofers in the distance, I turned on my own speakers, *climbed* back into my computer screen, and returned to the groove.

San Antonio was the twenty-fifth episode of the same thing. Two months of mounting the stage for ten thousand people and then climbing back into my makeshift studio in the RV to record new music.

Throw in a couple of summer award shows and galas, and you have a content-creating machine!

Videos of me leaping under dramatic stage lights surrounded by a wave of concertgoers jumping in step with me.

Pictures of me confidently posing with two more trophies to give my mom in lieu of grandbabies.

Clips on the RV as gospel legends like Kirk Franklin and Marvin Winans dropped in to record or listen to my works in progress.

On the "off" days, I would pause to appreciate the week's online engagement—the posts, the likes, the comments, the chatter. And, yeah, outwardly I was *doing well*. It became glaringly clear, though, that *doing well* didn't fill me nearly as much as *doing well* drained me. My flame was losing oxygen. Deep down I knew that. I had known that for a year—or four.

Have you ever felt like, despite the applause, or the accolades, or the accomplishments, the energy coming in was not matching the level of energy going out? Have you ever felt like your work, regardless of how productive it was, still wasn't *producing* or allowing a stable, energetic, or fulfilled life for you?

Welcome.

You're not alone.

Don't Be like Hamilton

There was a time when I judged people in high places, like celebrities and famous pastors. I judged the CEOs who couldn't keep their homes together. I judged the artists who blew up in front of people. I judged the actors who found themselves in the tabloids every year. When someone clearly lives at a higher altitude, accumulating more money, more access, more fame, more perks, more applause, and more influence than the average human, you kind of can't wait for life to prove that they are no better than you. So, every headline, every conspiracy theory, and every rumor is like fresh meat to a hungry wolf. And yup, that was me—a hungry wolf.

But I've gotten older. I've spent important years developing as an adult in front of people. I now know that most of those climbers—like most of us—aren't terrible, loose people. Most just get tired and are trying to survive.

Have you ever seen *Hamilton*? At a certain point in the Broadway musical about the former American statesman, the main character, Alexander Hamilton, has a streak of sleepless, work-filled nights. "You'd never seen a bastard orphan more in need of a break," Hamilton defensively croons as he unsuccessfully attempts to fight temptation.[1] His "break" ultimately comes in the form of cheating on his wife with a Miss Maria Reynolds after falling for her sob story. Hamilton couldn't—didn't—take a break, so *he* broke instead.

I could relate.

I told a friend over lunch that this part of *Hamilton* always stood out to me because, while many would only see Hamilton's character flaws and infidelity, I noticed his exhaustion. He got so far up in the clouds, with mounting political pressure, workload, and distance from his wife, that he became vulnerable to making a mistake, albeit a big one, that I'd like to think he would have avoided in simpler times.

"Bro, you have to write a book about that!" my friend exclaimed with his mouth agape. "I'll call my publisher now. They will love you."

Within days I was on a video conference call with the publishing team. They asked me if I had any ideas on book concepts. I initially pitched a risqué, gotcha-type book where

I challenged some of the lessons we Christians were (sometimes unintentionally) taught growing up. I don't think I even had any good examples yet. I just figured they were out there, and I'd find them when I needed to. The group nodded with some intrigue, but they also seemed to shudder at the thought of coming in so hot. That idea was from my head. It felt marketable and trendy and would be apropos for this post-church, online-service, church-hurt generation.

It wasn't from my heart, though.

My *heart* was trying to figure out why I knew great men and scandal-free men, but the overlap was rare—why I knew professionally successful women and happy women, but rarely did I find both in the same person. My heart was trying to figure out why the best of times professionally always seemed to come with the worst of times personally.

That reality seemed inescapable for me. A boon in my career always accompanied a dent on my heart. Hard, productive upward moves in my professional life came with less patience and joy, and more frustration, sin, and guilt in my personal life. Why did I get weaker as my résumé got stronger? Why did the grind make me feel less grounded? Wasn't work supposed to produce a proper, pleasant, and powerful life?

Consider this yourself. Do you live in a manner that puts pressure on work and achievement to acquire happiness and satisfaction? Have you ever imagined if you did well enough, made enough, or climbed high enough, there'd be an oasis up there?

There's Nothing Wrong with Climbing

I come from a world of grinders. My friends own companies, direct movies, run nonprofits, win Grammys, lead families, and build churches. Some have their journeys underlined by Jesus and Kingdom objectives, but even they aren't immune to a tinge of self-centered ambition and therefore stretch just a little further to be or stay great. All of us who reach to achieve great things get to a point where we realize the heights we are reaching for—and the intense ways in which we reach—come at the expense of something basic but incredibly integral to life. Often it's peace, or faith, or friends. Sometimes it's joy, energy, and vitality. It's as if our hard work takes us up a rugged mountain that only gets more and more uninhabitable the higher we go. To make matters worse, we then lose access to a less glamorous but sustaining and nutritious valley.

Every moment that our career, our grind, our assignment, and even our ministry is the center of our attention and priority, we push higher and higher up our "mountain"—a mindset of grinding, hustling, achieving, accomplishing, beating, maintaining, earning accolades, and acquiring titles. Most of us have a mountain. Every moment we try to escape mediocrity, win, defy expectations, avoid being broke, or survive, we climb higher and higher up our individual mountain. Whether it's external pressures, childhood trauma, and your kids, fans, contracts, or public scrutiny, it can all push us up the mountain. But here's the thing: We ultimately *do* have control over our mountain. Believe it or not, we can exist apart from it.

There's nothing wrong with climbing. There's nothing wrong with earning. Or acquiring. Or accomplishing. The mission will require some grind, some competition, and some hustle. Awards and promotions may be our portion too.

The problem arises when we live a life governed by the mountain, isolated on the mountain, with an identity created by the mountain. Friends encourage it. Culture mandates it. We may claim an all-consuming faith and wish for an all-consuming peace (like the one Christianity promises), but we consume ourselves with this big, rocky, leafless mountain anyway, unable to participate in the faith—or the peace—very often.

And we stay up there.

We *live* on this mountain. From the time we wake up in the morning to the time we try everything we can to fall asleep at night, we drown in thoughts about the mountain—bookings, work, homework, legwork, setup, takedown, and the pursuit of *greater*. And whether we want it to or not, it pushes us farther up into the clouds. We have this notion that with enough work, enough success, we will eventually arrive at a height called "happiness." Tal Ben-Shahar, author and psychologist, called it the "arrival fallacy."[2] The anticipation of this joyful oasis just one hundred feet *farther up* the mountain energizes us to continue climbing, but the success we eventually do garner never meets the hype.

The mountain is a part of life, but there is very little life on it.

There is another place to plant your flag.

There is a less heralded place where we must only be sons and daughters. Our responsibility is to remember—or discover—who we are without the man-made titles and rest in the divine title we were born again with. Below thousands of feet of ego, restlessness, self-centeredness, fear, and skewed memory is a valley full of everything you need for life.

> The mountain is a part of life, but there is very little life on it.

We rarely see the valley depicted in a positive light, but the one I speak of is a mindset of rest, restoration, rejuvenation, and perspective-keeping. It's where our true, core identity as son or daughter of God is fed.

Wherever you are in your climb, whether starting out or nearing burnout, it's about time we got honest and thorough about what comes with the pursuit and the maintenance of success. It isn't just about "balancing" your mountain time with a vacation or a church service. This isn't simply about labor versus rest—or work versus play.

It's about living from, gleaning from, and being defined by the identity, strength, and permission you get from the valley. Without that healthy perspective, you'll die prematurely doing something you once loved and that God once breathed on.

Before we go any higher—work any harder, dream any bigger, push any more intensely, or sacrifice any more—let's be more conscious of what we are getting ourselves into . . . and what has gotten into us.

CHAPTER 1

HOW'D YOU GET SO HIGH ANYWAY?

That year had beaten me to a pulp. I'd traveled thirty thousand miles in that RV and another one hundred thousand miles in the air.

And not to a resort with sand and sea.

I was traveling for work. Or traveling to keep LA from feeling so far away from the people I love in Chicago and DC.

I toured, but I was also producing an album, and while that has its daily triumphs and endorphin shots, those only come after long hours of mental toil.

My dad was dying of an aggressive neurological disorder, which punched a slowly leaking hole in my tires. I'd never enjoyed anything close to a robust relationship with him, so as his life slipped away, my hopes of ever having a "real" father were dying too.

Ironically, at the same time, I had three or four very close loved ones who needed me to fill in the gaps their own fathers had left.

Not whining. Just telling you what was going on.

But this night was supposed to be a good night. A bachelor doesn't get too many chances to come home to a woman and a meal.

That night, I would.

I was temporarily living on the chilly East Coast to pretend like I could act in a surprisingly impressive Christmas musical. That particular day of rehearsal had been long and challenging, but an unexpected text gave me something to look forward to. My girlfriend promised she'd beat my road manager and me back to the Airbnb and make beef stew. She had watched me make my version before and felt she could replicate—or even upgrade—it. She's a *much* better cook than I'll ever be, so she had my full confidence.

My road manager, who accompanies me to most shows and rehearsals, was tired, too, so at the first chance, we darted out of rehearsal. As we drove away from the auditorium, I could already taste the potatoes and carrots that were simmering on the stove. Thirty minutes later, I shuffled into the Airbnb, with low energy but high hopes. I threw my bag and coat carelessly onto the couch, shook off the Maryland winter, and dragged myself to the kitchen.

And there, your boy's heart was broken.

This beef "stew" that she'd prepared, well, it wasn't stew at all. It was soup. Just soup. Broth everywhere. The beef was drowning in it. And the carrots and potatoes I'd smelled from miles away were cut so small I could barely see them.

I know I'm being dramatic and bratty here, but the wings I flew home on, the savior of my day, was the anticipation of this *stew*!

But this was soup. Maybe even good soup. But *not stew*. It was *stoup*.

And as crazy, spoiled, and first-world as this sounds, I broke.

Instead of showing appreciation, I criticized my girlfriend's hard work. She responded by criticizing my criticism. And before I knew it, I was playing an angry symphony of high, screeching notes and colorful language. Enough to drive my roadie to the other side of the house. My girlfriend eventually had enough of the cacophony, too, and soon stormed out and drove away.

I left the *stoup* on the stove and stewed over how they'd deserted me at the first sign of me breaking down.

Didn't I deserve their long-suffering and grace? Of all people, *they* should know how much I had taken on that year and how much of myself I had given to the world. (And how much I had given to *them*!) How dare they not just stay and endure my wrath?

I had alienated two of my favorite humans when I needed them the most.

The stoup didn't ruin the night—I did.

If career and ministry were a mountain, I had climbed up quite a long way over the past few years, searching, sometimes sinfully, for some warmth and connection. But instead of enjoying friends, which is what I wanted and needed, I was cold and alone. Again.

I wasn't even mad that they'd left me in my tantrum. I was jealous. I was jealous that they could distance themselves from me and my life, but I couldn't. I was jealous that my burden was only mine. No one would ever know how heavy it was. No one was required to help me carry it up. And no one had to listen to my sad song from the summit.

With more salt, garlic, baby carrots, and a few more potatoes, I took a moment to salvage the stoup in the now-quiet kitchen. As I ate in silence, I felt the struggles . . . the triumphs . . . the failures of the year catch up to me. Maybe even a few years' worth of those. I recalled all the punches I'd absorbed, the awkward moments I'd smiled through, and the weights I'd quietly carried on my shoulders.

> I realized I had been climbing for years—and now I was choking alone in the high altitude.

Within minutes, my head got heavy, my heart raced, and my breath was hard to come by. My thoughts vacillated between past failures and future drains. I realized I had been climbing for years—and now I was choking alone in the high altitude. I felt like this *mountain* that I'd been living on was starting to kill me.

It's All in Your Head

Remember, the "mountain" represents our pursuit of success and progress toward that success. It's a frame of mind continually pointed toward achievement and accomplishment—more and higher. It can include one or more earthly assignments, God-given callings, or self-chosen career paths, but it is the mentality in which we work, chase, reach, and climb. Though we seem to aim for it, and wonder if others have reached it, experiencing an ultimate "mountaintop" is rare because even when we ascend to the peak of an endeavor—get the degree, break the record, make the numbers, create the family, rack up the followers—we tend to find another reason and route to climb.

This mountain doesn't represent your level of success. Whether you accomplish a lot or fail, living on the mountain—more precisely, living with a mountain *mindset*—has everything to do with your mild to obsessive preoccupation with success. The "mountain mindset" is one consumed with achieving, attaining, and maintaining wealth, position, and success. It's all in your head. There are plenty of people who have not had much visible success but are still fixated on achievement and are therefore actively climbing the mountain, but with little to show for it. In an ideal world, you and I would be the exact opposite: highly fruitful but not unhealthily tied to the slopes.

The hike up my mountain looked like thousands of hours of meticulous recording and editing, thousands of hours of graphic design and video editing, thirty-city tours with long meet and greets at each stop, thousands of miles of travel, thousands of hugs, millions of selfies, thousands of selfie redos, hundreds of interviews, several months on set, countless nights of abject loneliness, thousands of criticisms in

280 characters or less, stalkers, harassment, strained friendships, invasion of privacy, and public misinformation—all that to create and promote less than an hour of recorded music. Sometimes we climb so neurotically that we never count the cost and evaluate the toll the mountain has taken on our mind and body. And by "we," I mean *me*.

So in that random Airbnb—bowl of stoup in hand—after years on my mountain, there I was, wondering if my energy, sacrifice, and talent had given me a worthwhile return. I knew I'd never have a clear answer if I kept climbing. I needed to figure out a way to get off—before I fell off.

> Pastor, I'm sorry for texting you this late, but I just wanted to tell you myself I have to cancel. You know I love you and everyone [at your church]. I just literally feel like I'm breaking down. Never been here before. I've been nonstop, but the doctor visits are starting to pile up and the outbursts are becoming frequent. I feel like I'm going to implode. Please forgive me! This isn't normal. And I don't know what I would've had to give to you guys. I will make it up to you ASAP. I just have to try something. I have to try stopping . . . (December 13 at 1:07 a.m.)

This was the first of many texts and calls that would go out over the next few days. I felt officially burnt out. All I could think of was clearing the deck. Canceling everything felt like professional suicide, but so did running the risk of a more public "stoup" incident.

That December, for the first time, I chose to ditch the mountain. I chose to resist my impulse to climb. Money was lost. Good press was lost. My delusion of invincibility was lost. Some colleagues questioned my dependability. I felt like I was letting everyone down. But everything in my soul—and in my lower back and eyes and head—said I needed to stop.

This burnout wouldn't be resolved with just physical rest either. I had disconnected with *why* I was climbing in the first place. Whatever I had set out to find on this mountain, five thousand feet in the air, I hadn't found it yet.

But *He* Started It!

I remember the first day God showed me my mountain.

During my first two years of undergrad at Columbia College in Chicago, I spent most of the time between classes writing and recording songs in my dorm room. Before freshman year officially started, I had maxed out my first credit card—with a limit of $800—to squeeze out a $400 HP laptop, an audio interface, and a couple of good speakers. By the following summer, I could afford a few seven-by-four-foot cuts of OSB plywood and mattress foam for a makeshift vocal booth. And by the start of my second year, I felt ready to do some professional(ish) recording.

A few months into the fall semester, I had about six or seven songs I was proud of. Christmas was coming, and

I had the typical amount of money most college students have: *none*.

Remember blank CDs? And burning? And blank CD labels? For a week after Thanksgiving, I recorded personal messages for every aunt and uncle, my sister and mom, printed out an unimpressive inkjet label, and burned those songs to a CD. I slid each one into a CD sleeve (remember CD sleeves?) and became the star of the McReynolds Christmas of 2008.

For the next couple of school years, as friends rolled in and out of my dorm room, they'd plead for a copy of that EP to take home. For this young songwriter, producer, and artist in the making, my music was never exactly "ready" for public release. I probably turned the volume of the guitars—or the drums, or the background vocals—up or down thirty times, but by the summer after junior year, I finally started to give in to their friendly demands. Corey, a dynamic singer in his own right, who tours with me to this day, was among those original copy holders.

Corey would regularly play the EP in his car. Some days, he'd assist his pastor, Pastor Sean, with errands around the city, and Sean was particularly taken by the fresh sound. Corey offered his copy to Sean and days later, the pastor took his portable CD player (remember . . . never mind) to the health club. There, he saw a friend, fellow clergyman Pastor John Hannah, on the treadmill and asked him if he had ever heard of me or my music. Now, that must have been one of the more expensive portable CD players with the *45-second electronic skip protection*, for Hannah to be able to listen without his jog disrupting the flow.

Pastor Hannah was just as impressed as Sean, so Corey's CD was passed on once again. This particular chain of custody would've been no big deal, except Pastor Hannah's day job was working as a radio announcer for the morning-commute gospel radio show—the most popular in the state of Illinois.

One morning, I woke up to my phone annoyingly vibrating on my pillow. The sun was out, and my bedroom lights were still on. I'd obviously passed out in the middle of working on music.

I had been staying at my mom's apartment to save money on senior year housing, but she had already left for the day, so I awoke to bright silence. My eyes bristled at the daylight streaming through the window on one side of the bed, so I flipped over to brave the lamplight until my eyes adjusted. As my eyes focused on my cell phone, I saw I had missed about ten texts and five calls. That's not incredibly abnormal for a young musician who typically wakes up at noon after a long night of working, but it was only 9:00 a.m.! *What's going on?* I wondered.

As soon as I opened the most recent text, another call came through. A lady I'd met only a few months before at a local music workshop abruptly shouted, "Take this number down! I need you to call into the radio station. They are asking for you!" She rattled off the number while I struggled to even understand why I was in trouble. She said, "Hannah played your song! Call in!"

Apparently, Pastor Hannah had snuck one of my songs into the normally rigid radio playlist and implored the entire city of Chicago to ask me to call in if they, in fact, knew this "Jonathan McReynolds guy."

After first teasing me for my "pillow voice"—it took me years to shake off my reputation among radio hosts as a non-morning person—Hannah praised the music and invited me to sing at his five-thousand-member church.

And just like that, I had my first radio spin and my first professional booking.

It had all started with a low-budget Christmas gift! But God used it to give me a mountain.

My career began without my deliberately igniting it. Those next months, it seemed my cell phone vibrated with good news every morning. It was strange. Divine. I will never claim to fully understand why and how my life turned out this way, but one thing was obvious: God started it.

God has a way of starting stuff. You look up and, suddenly, the conditions seem to be perfect for a new job, a new love, or a new pursuit. It's because the conditions were orchestrated. God wants us to succeed, ascend, connect, and expand. We can say with reasonable certainty that pursuing goals, reaching higher heights, and succeeding in some way is a *part* of God's plan for each of our lives.

I will never claim to fully understand why and how my life turned out this way, but one thing was obvious: God started it.

First Kings 2:3 says if you "walk in obedience to him, and keep his decrees and commands, his laws and regulations . . . you may prosper in all you do and wherever you go."

Proverbs 16:3 says, "Commit to the LORD whatever you do, and he will establish your plans."

The prerequisite is fearing and obeying the Lord, but Psalm 128:2 says those who do "will eat the fruit of your labor; blessings and prosperity will be yours."

The Parable of the Ten Minas (Luke 19:11–27) and the Parable of the Talents (Matthew 25:14–30) don't solely encourage proper use of your resources, time, and energy; the parables also frown upon leaving potential untapped, practicing lackluster stewardship, and neglecting to use, invest, and multiply what God has provided.

Look at how much credit God takes for giving Solomon wisdom, prospering Joseph in Egypt, conquering Israel's military enemies, protecting Job's assets, and rapidly expanding the early Church.

Mountains can be gorgeous, honorable, world-changing, Kingdom-expanding, God-pleasing missions. Mountains don't lie about their heights, their rough terrain, or their thin air, though. Mountains are, well, mountains. I think we just do a bad job of keeping them in perspective, without the extra glamour and romance.

What is your mountain?

The climb may be a professional one. The climb may be in social stature or class. The climb may be a new ministry you're growing.

Every climb is distinct, but some things characterize them all: The higher up you go, the more that threatens to separate you from your original and most real identity as a son or daughter of God. We can become so "boss," so "king," so "queen," so "worker," and so "entrepreneur" that we lose touch with the "son" or "daughter" within us.

The mountain offers us new titles, new responsibilities, and new business. There is money to be made on the mountain. There is publicity on the mountain. There are pats on the back and applause on the mountain. There are likes and attention and ego-feeding. And it's that incredible benefits package that seduces us into making the mountain home. Being *crowned by the climb* seems like the more glorious, sexier, even safer marker for your existence. That honor can be misleading, though. You may get to the highest heights in what you *do*, but end up farther from the world below that kept you aware of who you *are*. And after all, "What good will it be for someone to gain the whole world, yet forfeit their soul?" (Matthew 16:26).

While I am 100 percent certain that God started my trek on this mountain, the puzzling part of all this is that the climb took so much out of me and even pulled me *away* from Him at times. We think the awesome task is climbing the mountain, being great, and changing the world. The *most* awesome task is climbing the mountain God instructs us to without letting it change our core relationship with and identity in Him.

Fear and Ego Tend to Take Over

The song that first got played on the radio was more about my uncertainty and indecisiveness with Christ than it was about how well things were going with Him.

Lord I'm split in two,
Part of me loves the world and the other loves you.
So what do I do?
I wanna be saved, but I gotta stay cool too.[1]

My song "No Gray" eventually speaks to the *high Christian standard* I felt I must live up to and how God wanted me to rise to the occasion. Somehow, a song full of ambivalence pushed me onto a pedestal of authority—authority I thought I was admitting I didn't have. The song convicted people in such a fresh way, and it quickly turned me into a "gospel artist," a symbol of purity and holiness, and, well . . . a minister. (Which is quite ironic, considering the songs were generally inspired by sinful college nights. Talk about imposter syndrome!)

Right when I became an adult and started my walk with Christ, I was also suddenly a professional artist and a minister of His message. By God's grace, I handled it OK. Thousands, then millions were touched. No huge scandals, though there was certainly plenty of sin. Either way, I had never been an adult without being a singer, never been a singer without being a Christian, and never been a Christian without being some sort of leader in the Christian world.

Adult. Christian. Singer. Minister. I never knew one without the other.

More precisely, as soon as I was becoming conscious of being God's son, I became one of God's servants. One of His spokesmen. One of His Church's leaders. I was honored—still am—that God had enough confidence in me to give me a mountain and push me to His front lines. But I think I did a poor job of distinguishing what was intended for me and what was for me to give to the world. I turned my prayers into songs before I said "Amen." I put His answers to music before I let them permeate my heart and change my mind. My imposter syndrome intensified my fuss over the mountain, so even as I encouraged others to embrace a "valley" of love, stillness, and worship, the professional growth only pushed me farther up. I released the best parts of my relationship with God, even the parts that were meant to edify *me*.

And I did this for years. From album to album, church to church, tour to tour, gaining fans and press and attention. Learning a lesson and writing about it. Cutting myself open in interviews just to encourage their audience. The extra pressure pushed me farther up the mountain. And while that first song never got a music video, there would be many, many music videos for my songs to come.

Obsessed with "Up"

Don't all guys, at some point, imagine being part of a boy band? Whether it's Backstreet Boys or Boyz II Men, I don't know a guy who doesn't fancy a little bit of that cheesy swagger and all the screaming fans. One day, on the set of a music video shoot, I had my chance. I had the outfit—too much leather. I had the dramatic lighting. And I went for it.

I'm just inviting You in my situation.
Come thru 'cause I need You in my situation.

This song was derived from a prayer my close friend had prayed during a very dire and worrisome moment. Though we don't always know how things *should* end up, we have faith that God's presence in the problem is better than any solution we'd ever think up. It's a serious song, but as the cameras zoomed in and out, I felt like being a little goofy. I assumed the classic boy band stance, smized longingly into the shadows, and pointed directly at the camera lens as I mouthed, "I'm just inviting You in my situation."

Did you catch my grave mistake? Let's backtrack.

Temptations-esque poses? Classic.

Intense gaze into the camera? Engaging.

That point toward the camera, though? Shameful!

It has been formally established that to properly refer to God, you must point *up*! The Christian delegation had this meeting at Azusa or one of Billy Graham's crusades and agreed on this. There's no room for negotiation. (Just joking—kinda.)

When humans talk about God, we motion up. We associate *up* with the divine, the powerful, and the heroic. We build towers to get closer to the gods; we build pedestals to distinguish us from the ordinary folk; we pay millions of dollars more for the house high on the awkward slope than we do for the one firmly planted at the bottom of the hill. Or is that just LA?

The point is, *up* is where we all want to be, after this life and during it. We are obsessed with *up*. We study, schmooze, perform, organize, produce, create, and promote our way up this mountain, hoping that one day our mothers will be proud and our exes will be jealous. Even when God gives us a mountain to climb, an assignment to fulfill, an industry to lead, he never asks us to *obsess* over our ascent. We do because, well, we *add* to His commission.

And I saw that all toil and all achievement spring from one person's envy of another. This too is meaningless, a chasing after the wind. (Ecclesiastes 4:4)

Tell us how you really feel, King Solomon!

The whole book of Ecclesiastes reads as if this king of Israel is aggravatedly trying to figure out why he spent so much time and energy devoting himself to hard work and wisdom. (You can tell by how many times he screams, "*Meaningless!*")

Before Solomon was born, he was destined to be king. And before he was king, he was chosen to construct the temple. *God started it!* His major life mountains were set out for him early on. But we can tell he may have had an extra unhealthy devotion to the climb because that entire book is a rather miserable yet familiar journey of counting the costs and benefits of his approach to life.

In chapter 2, the king revealed that he spent lots of time and energy undertaking "great projects" (Ecclesiastes 2:4), building houses, planting vineyards, amassing "silver and gold for [him]self," a harem of women, and an in-house cover band (2:8). Now, one may ask, how much of that did God demand, and how much did Solomon just feel compelled to do? And why was he compelled to do it?

Somewhere along the way, we convince ourselves that we need the prestige, status, and honor of the mountain. Our value sneakily attaches to our ability to continually achieve, continually impress, or continually stay above reproach. Yes, that's how the *world* works, but that conditional status and performance-based value is tough on the soul.

The applause I've gotten for my good works does not feed a heart that is built to be loved apart from them.

God rewards His servants in several ways, even in this life. But His joy, His presence, His favor, His company are harder to notice when you're consumed by your own ambition and survival on the mountain. There is a beauty and an order that King Solomon eventually finds in how God fashioned this world. He just wasn't going to find it obsessed with and constrained by his mountain.

CHAPTER 2

BE HONEST ABOUT THE MOUNTAIN

It was great to be at the top, but it's better to be home.
—Dave Roskelley

Dave Roskelley, a plucky engineer from Chicago, enjoys "doing difficult things." He has devoted fifteen years of disposable time and income to climbing the highest peaks in the world. Roskelley is known for climbing the tallest mountain of each continent and being the first American to ascend the tallest volcanic summits of each continent. While conquering these incredible heights excites him, he never minimizes the pain, adversity, and terror that await him every hundred feet into the sky. There is a refreshing dichotomy to him: a profound drive to climb but also an understanding that "humans aren't engineered to operate in those kinds of environments."[1]

Professional mountain climbers know the joys of reaching the impossible. The ecstasy of a summit and the adrenaline from conquering obstacles along the way.

Professional climbers also know that the actual process of climbing . . . sucks.

The climbers who conquer the likes of Everest and Kilimanjaro, like Roskelley, prepare themselves for the inclement weather, the lack of sustenance, and the constant danger of falling that await. They pack heavy clothes, extra food and water, and all the carabiners, crampons, and ice axes they can carry to anchor themselves securely to the mountain. These *real* mountaineers are well-armed for the standard mountain issues they know they will face. They know the mountain is a place of honor, but also a place of hunger. They understand that much is to be conquered and earned, but plenty is lost in the process.

Yet the "climbers" I know in everyday life, from public figures to high school teachers, don't always seem to acknowledge that reality. Roskelley, having conquered several difficult peaks around the world, now knows that the mountain can only be his temporary mission. And that his real home is much lower to the ground. Our society, however, is full of everyday climbers who forget there is more.

One such climber married young but handled it well and climbed up to become a model family man. In his generation, where Black men often took a more distant and irresponsible route, he chose to climb toward integrity and duty. He pushed for his CPA certification and established a career, a family home, and a marriage of several decades. Solid success has brought him to a high, flat place on his mountain. You might call it a *plateau*. His days may no longer be consumed with attaining higher heights, but he still actively works to maintain life at the height to which he has climbed. While he is not self-righteous or arrogant, all that nobility and valor, all the self-denial and sacrifice have become his most protected sources of identity. So he stands defensively on his plateau. Never visibly shaken, his stress is internalized and manifests as stomach ulcers. He believes in prayer, but when you are known for standing tall, sometimes it's hard to be seen on your knees. When you're known for always smiling, it's scary to be seen crying out to God. He may want to rush to the altar to bare his soul, but not in front of the congregation. So instead, he remains on the mountain—not knowing if he'd still be himself if he ever came down.

Another one of my favorite climbers is a lady of faith known for her wisdom, brilliance, beauty, and talent. She has climbed to the highest peaks of her art form. The people who know her, revere her. With impact and respect resembling a mega-pastor, encouraging people to go to the "valley" of self-love, unity, and mindfulness ironically pushed her up, *out of* the valley, higher up her mountain. Up where she lives, in rarefied air, she has her choice of love interests but none of them hit the mark for long. Staying up on the summit, like a goddess—away from autographs, tabloids, and rumors—costs her companionship and some peace. But to her, it certainly beats risking being seen and judged up close in her mere human form.

Both the accountant and the artist have traveled fruitfully up their mountains.

Both need some time off their mountains.

Fatherhood, adulthood, celebrity, success, whatever pursuit—or climb—we're called to can make us feel like we can't come down to the lowly valley, even if that is where nourishment and freedom reside. Instead of risking the trip back down, humbling ourselves in front of our admirers and our haters, and losing what we think is our value, we train ourselves to live on less. Less food, less oxygen, less company, and, yes, less God.

Natural things like raw talent, peer pressure, competition, and the expectations of others can push you up the mountain. Spiritual things like a divine calling can push you up there. Bad things can push you up there. Good things can push you up there. Life has millions of ways of pushing you further and further into that grinding, achieving *mountain* mindset.

Professional mountain climbers know the mountain is a rewarding place to be. They also know there are standard mountain issues they must prepare for. Perhaps we can learn from them as we deal with the cold of isolation and lack of intimacy, the lack of spiritual food, and the constant threat of falling off.

Those standard mountain issues beg some standard mountain questions. Let's start with three.

Is Anybody with Me up Here?

Interviewer: Judging from the pictures you have
provided for us, when you ascended Mount

Everest, you did so with a long string of
about 100–200 people that were going up all
at the same time. And yet you mentioned in
previous engagements that when you're on the
mountain, you're on your own. It's every man
for himself. Do you really feel like you're all
alone in a crowd like that?

Roskelley: You do, because everybody is operating,
really, at the limits of their ability . . . if you
have a problem, everyone is in the same boat.

While Roskelley climbed his mountain, pursuing his
greatest feat yet, hundreds of people were technically along-
side him. He was not alone, but it felt as if he were because
everyone was working at the "limits of their ability," less
able to create, nurture, or appreciate community. When
everyone is operating like this, isolation is the result.

Maybe you don't even notice when you're operating at
an elevated level. I can't tell you how many times my doctor has observed high stress levels in me, and when asked
about them, I realized I felt no different than normal.
Unfortunately, like me, climbers are often so used to the high
output and effort that they forget it's actually, well, high.
Even though we do it with smiles on our faces, the jumpers
are always trying to jump higher, the shy are always trying
to be bold, the awkward are always trying to be sexy, the
students are always trying to be masters. The unchurched
are building a church, the unfathered are learning to father.

Everyone on the mountain is operating toward the limits of their ability. That grind, that focus, requires some level of self-absorption, some level of fixation. And that hyperfocus commonly pulls us away from the company of friends, pushing us into isolation.

So, we can't rely on the mountain to provide friends.

But can we at least keep the ones we have?

Not all the time.

There weren't too many Bible characters who got to go up the mountain with their crew.

Elijah went up Mount Horeb to rethink the risk and reward of his mission in Israel—and he did it in seclusion.

Moses came down with the Ten Commandments but certainly went up his mountain alone.

Joseph's mountain took him through Potiphar's house, prison, and the Egyptian palace. None of his family or friends were said to be there for the ride.

Everyone can't go up with you. Very few people are graced to climb the unique mountain you're climbing. Very few people must. Everyone isn't married with kids. Everyone isn't trying to be the CEO of a Fortune 500 company. Everyone doesn't want a Grammy. And, frankly, everyone isn't trying to be excellent at something. That means the more you ascend into the clouds—naturally—the fewer familiar faces you will see.

One of the first and biggest surprises to me as I began to climb was that the mountain was not nearly as crowded and friendly as it looked on TV. Can you relate? While accomplishing the extraordinary was the goal, I wasn't completely prepared to miss out on some of the ordinary things—like company. It gets cold on the mountain and without the warmth of comforting people, you are bound to feel the chill of loneliness.

To make matters worse, as we climbers turn inward, gaining momentum but losing people, we tend to deal with the cold loneliness by climbing more. We spend—I spent—more time in front of the computer, more time creating content, more time practicing our instruments and thinking of ways to take over the world. This *movement* is the only thing that seems to keep our blood circulating. We work harder, climb higher, and bury ourselves in our companies, ministries, and audition tapes just to make it worth the lonely frostbite. Yes, oddly enough, the cold isolation of the mountain normally pushes us farther up it. We tend to look at pausing our work to go back down to warmer, friendlier pastures as quitting. So we end up farther from what we truly need.

Each time you left your girlfriend to study, told the guys no because of work, or chose to stay inside to avoid the paparazzi (Just me? Fine!), you were likely being influenced by the mountain and the isolation it requires. It may have been a necessary choice, a wise choice. But it's an isolating choice nonetheless. A choice that we have to live with.

Isolation is not always a bad thing. And let me reiterate: *Climbs* are not an inherently bad thing. Being on the mountain is an honor, and it's often the assignment. God *uses* isolation too. The Spirit literally led Jesus into the wilderness so He could succeed where Adam failed—against temptation. Isolation is a common and often necessary part of every prophet's, pastor's, president's, parent's, and pioneer's life.

It is *not* supposed to be a *permanent* condition, though. Surviving a season of isolation may prove you are strong enough for the climb, but it doesn't prove you're built to live at that altitude forever. No amount of greatness, responsibility, anointing, or purpose demands that you must be apart from people *forever*.

Yet climbers—often unintentionally—choose that life of isolation all the time.

Can Anybody Really See Me?

I remember being onstage in Dallas, Texas, during our My Truth tour. My team and I had been singing for an hour and were in a very physically demanding part of the show. We were ten cities into the tour at this point, and I was dog-tired. Still dancing, singing, and leading, but dog-tired. As we danced, I looked at the audience and tried to think of a cute way to tell them I was exhausted. The oblivious crowd cheered us on, reveling in the beautiful Pentecostal chaos they were a part of.

So instead, I looked around at my background singers and gave *them* the "I'm tired" look, but they, similar to the audience, only smiled back and jigged harder. They're still in their twenties. For five years, I taught a gospel class at my alma mater, Columbia College, and one of the singers was an old student of mine. Point is, they had twice the energy to spare.

I thought in that moment, *I wonder if anyone even sees that I'm tired.*

The audience wouldn't guess it. My singers couldn't react to it. I wondered if I'd ever be met where I was. That is, seen for how I actually felt or perhaps who I was at any given moment.

Mountain life is full of moments where you wonder if you'll ever be met where you are.

Even in a room full of people who endeavor to show you love, something is still missing.

I've talked to many obsessive climbers who don't feel *seen.* Sound familiar? Being seen is being understood. Being seen is being understood deeply. Being seen is being understood deeply without constantly having to provide extra context or translation. Being seen means no one is looking down at your life or up at your life. But on a mountain, you may feel like almost everyone is looking at you, your actions, your words, and your life from above or below. Mountain life does not always give ample opportunity to be seen from a level, objective perspective.

> Mountain life is full of moments where you wonder if you'll ever be met where you are.

Have you ever felt like no matter how high the platform, how grand the stage, or how respected the position, somehow you're still invisible? People are obviously seeing and responding to your gift, your title, or your product, but do you feel they are seeing *you*? And do you ever wonder if the reason they cannot see you is because of that glorious gift or title—and how much you've invested into the climb?

Loved and needed, but not seen—certainly a standard mountain issue.

Or perhaps we're seen, but from a skewed perspective.

That moment onstage made me realize that from a high place—onstage, on my mountain—I can't expect anyone to know how the climb is affecting me. Some won't care. Some won't be able to fathom it. Some relationships, some interactions, and some exchanges just won't be completely reciprocal. Sometimes we are meeting the needs of people who have no capacity or responsibility to reciprocate.

And it's not their fault.

God, please keep us from growing cold to all those people—congregants, employees, fans, and peers—who "love" us, demand from us, but cannot necessarily see us or give us what we need. And then teach us to recognize and appreciate when someone can see us and deliver.

The lack of intimacy, interpersonal understanding, and "feeling seen" is, for many of us, the worst part of the mountain. The pursuit and pressure of such a high altitude left me searching for warmth and cover in cold places. I looked for intimacy in risky places. I was temperamental with the ones who did their best to love me. I took random personality tests, sought counsel from Reverend Google, and fell down TikTok rabbit holes looking for a name for my condition—a name for this aloneness. I was charismatic but alone. Desired but alone. Surrounded but alone. If you're anything like me, chances are you aren't crazy or antisocial or hopelessly intimidating or off-putting. You simply have no clue how to come off your mountain and be *just* a son or daughter of God.

That is, be *just* human.

And feel human.

The mountain can be lonely and isolating, so staying stuck in the mountain mindset all the time will create an entire *life* that lacks intimacy. At that point, we pray our art, work, and ministries grow legs, arms, and lips so they can fill the spaces intended for human interaction.

Marriage may not be for you. A large group of vacation-ready friends may not be in the cards for you. And your social life may never be as it was freshman year of college. But there is very little evidence of God encouraging or sentencing any of us to a *life* of isolation or a *life* without intimacy, even if there is a season of it.

Want proof?

Adam was well on his way to a life without people, until God Himself said, "It is not good for the man to be alone" (Genesis 2:18).

"Is anybody with me?" and "Can anybody see me?" cannot stay heavy, unanswered questions forever. If the mountain is generally lonely and we aren't meant to be lonely forever, the mountain must not be where we are meant to spend all the days of our lives. There must be another place we can go. Another place we *should* go. Often.

Is There Anything to Eat?

Do yourself a favor and Google "The Alps" or "The Himalayas" or "The Rockies" and tell me if you see green at the tops of any of those mountains. The Rocky Mountains, in particular, show a perfect, gradual decline of vegetation as you move up the mountains. No matter how lush the bottom of the mountain may be, the top 80 percent looks to be completely devoid of life. Actually, that's not true. You will find one living thing at a height of 6,700 meters, or 22,000 feet: a spider. A Himalayan jumping spider. How do they survive? On flies that have been blown up by the wind from lower altitudes.[2]

At rising altitudes, there are fewer gas molecules in the air, which leads to what is called "thin air." Your lungs will have a tough time handling the lack of oxygen. One mountaineer compared climbing at high altitude to "running on a treadmill and breathing through a straw."[3] On Everest, the area above 26,000 feet is called the Death Zone. There is so little oxygen, the brain and lungs become starved for it. Stay there too long and your judgment will be impaired, and you will likely die. Unfortunately, this happens often. Because of overcrowding on Everest and gridlock while waiting to get to the top, in recent years, fatalities in the Death Zone have increased.[4] You can preach that message yourself!

Aside from the lack of oxygen, our stomachs will be angry too—there's *nothing to eat up there*. I mean, except for the spiders. And maybe salt from the rocks?

Scarcity—the lack of life-sustaining nutrition—is the second standard mountain issue. The climber who started—with all his health, sanity, and energy—is not the same climber after a few thousand feet.

As I started to travel more, my mother noticed the attention I'd get from celebrities—particularly some who would not immediately be thought of as believers. As we sat shocked at the public endorsements I was getting, my mother asked me, "Who do you think are the most forgotten souls in the Church?"

Unready for the question, I waited a beat, then said, "Probably the drug addicts, prostitutes . . ."

She laughed and said, "Well, we have plenty of outreach programs for them." And she was right. Our church spent a good portion of the summer passing out tracts to everyone hanging around the liquor store. Several night services were hijacked by the neighborhood troublemakers, intoxicated but clearly searching for the Lord.

She continued, "I actually think celebrities are."

I initially rebuffed that thought, as the modern Church world seemed to be way *too* focused on preferential treatment and coddling the rich and famous.

But on second thought, I realized my mother had a point—perhaps there was preferential treatment for the riches and fame, but it came at the expense of *proper* treatment for the actual soul. Years of drowning in scripts and red carpets, tours and recording sessions, books and classes can leave anyone high in their pursuit but with no time for or access to spiritual food. Humans—even the Church's humans—are very easily duped by outer appearances. And no one looks healthier and more divinely taken care of than the mountain climber who has acquired some level of success. We may be seen getting fat off the spoils of achievement, but without pure guidance, godly community, and faith-building input, the *inner man* who connects to God is wasting away. Our bank accounts may be fortified, our careers may be exploding, and our families may be "movin' on up." This skinny inner man, however? This soul obsessively climbing up a scarce mountain? Well, he's losing spiritual calories *and* resistance to the temptation and adversity that every human is bound to encounter.

New levels, new devils.

—Unknown

Pastor John Hannah, who gave me my first big radio spin and booking, was the first man I heard say it, so I'll credit him for that profound truth. As you climb to new levels of this barren mountain, the extra attention from the opposite sex, the stresses of more responsibility, the new money and status to manage, and the vultures that scan dry places for weakness can bring about new and exciting devils to battle.

From my experience, the climb can also weaken you to the *old* habits, people, and devils you thought you'd mastered. While the old missionaries from my home church might have worried that I'd pick up a new cocaine addiction on the way up, the truth is, the lust of my teenage years—women, *fine* women—just got more expressed and harder to ignore as I climbed. So often, at least for me, it was "new levels, same devils." German philosopher Friedrich Nietzsche said, "When we are tired, we are attacked by ideas we conquered long ago."[4] The mountain's scarcity is consistent, and our desires are cyclical. Therefore, our mistakes can easily become cyclical too. We abstain from sin and avoid error until we are hungry again.

Our corporate worlds run on Dunkin' more than they run on any kind of spiritual energy boosts. Our managers aren't necessarily trying to lead with godly love. Our quotas have nothing to do with our faith and peace, but everything to do with our production. Talent attracts angels *and* demons. Contrary to what a lot of Christians may think, the worlds of business, entertainment, academics, athletics, and even ministry-building pull on our work ethic, intelligence, charisma, risk-taking, brilliance, perseverance, and resilience just as much as—if not more than—they pull on our faith. On the mountain, we

> We abstain from sin and avoid error until we are hungry again.

can become known for our worldly productivity more than our spiritual fruit. So those become the muscles we flex, the muscles we strengthen. Those are our climbing muscles. And we tend to work them, without food, without rest, without fresh clarity or fresh inspiration, until we burn out.

The prophetic words don't come as often as they did at the beginning. There's no community covering us daily in prayer. Sabbaths and sabbaticals are less appealing, so rest—naturally, and in God's finished work—is harder to come by. All the things that geared us up for the climb, all the words that made us feel we could "run through troops," and all the faith-feeding fruit we could've eaten in another chapter of life are very hard to find.

Consequently, the "devils" of temptation, pride, greed, depression—altitude sickness, if you will—start to bother us a little bit more than they used to. Remember Hamilton's moment of weakness? The tired and the hungry are vulnerable. Some thoughts weren't even thoughts until you started climbing the mountain of marriage. An otherwise forgotten childhood trauma didn't affect you until the last promotion. The lights, the cameras, and the comments made you pay attention to your flaws more than ever before. And you don't have enough energy to really fight back. Those devils seem much stronger when you're out of food and out of air.

Next time you see a pastor fall, a celebrity stumble, or a mother lose her mind, don't assume they were on the edge from birth. More often than not, they are starving. Somebody get that person a plate! Some *real* prophetic encouragement. Some Scripture to chew on. Some clean music. The divine resources that humans are given to enjoy are rarely found on the mountain. We try to sustain the mountains way more than they try to sustain us.

And therein lies the big question: Should we expect our mountains to sustain us?

Do we expect fatherhood to sustain the father? Do we expect the career to always give us strength to pursue it? Do we expect stars to live off their stardom? Well, we shouldn't. The mountain has all it needs to remain a mountain, but it won't help you climb it. And it doesn't care whether you live or die, keep your faith or lose heart.

And What if I Fall?

One day, some Twitter (X) user ran across a recognizable actor from my childhood, Geoffrey Owens, working a much less grandiose job at Trader Joe's. In typical Twitter fashion, people around the world—most with similar or less-impressive jobs—took turns drooling over his apparent fall from stardom.

A good rags-to-riches movie inspires us and gives us tears of joy, but a seemingly sad riches-to-rags reality show feeds our insecure flesh. What ensued was a public mocking of a man who was "in the dark wood of unemployment and debt" just trying to "see if [he] could hang in there with [his] career."[5]

As a former resident of LA, I have seen firsthand the fragility of riches and the mortality of a good contract. There is a strong level of advocacy for the homeless population there, and I can't help but think it's because the entertainers of the city know they are often only a few unfruitful auditions away from suffering the same condition. To watch how the tweeting masses jeered him was thought-provoking. And cringeworthy. And upsetting. I highly doubt anyone climbing a noble mountain joined in the ignorant chorus because Geoffrey Owens seemed to be living our biggest nightmare.

Many nights, I've wondered what I would do if I somehow couldn't afford the lifestyle I have now. What if I had to sell some assets, or was struggling for bookings and demand? How could I descend the mountain once I found out I was no longer fit for it? How would I survive Uber-ing an old fan? How desperate would I look making cold calls to revive my career? What if my voice gave out and no one cared about me?

Those questions—ridiculous, spoiled, entitled, and elitist as they may be—are kind of normal for a climber. Many of us are always thinking of these worst-case scenarios and wondering what internal fortitude and external cooperation we will need to keep from falling into them. Lower heights leave more room for mistakes. You have less to lose. But the higher you climb, the more you guard against falling off the mountain.

Yeah, you guessed it. We've arrived at a third standard mountain issue. Your energy starts being spent on *not* losing the money you made. *Not* letting your kids down. *Not* getting bad press around the brand you built. *Not* getting fired. And all that anxiety certainly isn't good for you.

If the climb wasn't enough—the isolation, the lack of intimacy, and the scarcity—now you're further stressed about how you'll manage to stay in this unfriendly place. Our egos don't know if we could survive that embarrassment and that disappointment. We may say we just don't want to disappoint the fans, the consumers, and the wife. But

> But the higher you climb, the more you guard against falling off the mountain.

normally, we are most afraid of disappointing *ourselves* and losing the temporary value we feel the mountain gives us. If you're reading this book—beginning the climb, wanting the climb, years into the climb—chances are you aren't afraid of heights. It's that majestic view from the top that you're hoping for. It's the feeling of accomplishment and achievement that you want to experience. The thought of looking down at all the entry-level rookies you passed on the way up, or looking down at your daughter who thinks the world of you, or looking down at your adoring fans probably intrigues you. A mountain climber must have bravery and grit, a sense of adventure, and an interest in the widening world above and beneath them.

We don't normally have *acrophobia*, the fear of heights, but we still may have a healthy amount of *basophobia*. That is, the fear of falling. What could be scarier to a mountain climber than being seen somersaulting down the hill they've been posting about being on top of?

This crippling fear is conveniently pronounced "base-o-phobia," and we are indeed intensely afraid of ever again starting back at the base. What makes even walking back down scary is having to renavigate the craziness at the base—all the things and people we feel we have graduated from, all the vulnerability that could blemish our image, and all the virtues the mountain would eat for breakfast. If you fear a fall from your mountain would kill you, perhaps you've gotten too high. And I bet the "height" isn't real. It's a mindset. The mountain mindset.

This *Can't* Be Home

Interviewer: How many people live on Mt. Everest?
Roskelley: So, nobody actually lives there.

Sometime in 2021, when the COVID-19 pandemic was finally releasing its grip from our social lives, two of my guys invited me out of the house. On this cool summer night, I walked into a chic restaurant somewhere in Hollywood. Groups of model-type women and guys who want you to know they work out littered the moody scene. I scanned the room for a familiar face, kind of hoping I wouldn't find any besides the two I'd come for. I wasn't ready to be *that* social. (I rarely am.) After fifty feet of squeezing through candlelit tables and huddled drinkers, the room opened up to a beautiful terrace and I spotted my party just as they were sitting down.

Both of my guys also want people to know they work out. I rolled my eyes at the underutilization of their shirts' buttons. They knew I was judging them, even from twenty feet away. We laughed and I joined them at the table.

One guy has been a great friend and restaurant-touring partner for most of my time spent in LA. He's not the point here.

The other, however, was a very new acquaintance. Our careers in Christian art had kept us aware of each other for years, but the friendship was ironically beginning now that he'd given up the ministry and his faith altogether. The way I see it, like me, as soon as he hit his twenties, his immature relationship with Jesus, mixed with his very mature talents and poise, resulted in a *pre*mature release into the faith-based marketplace.

The pressure of the climb—business, ego, and people—sifted both of our faith journeys into their most marketable parts, and by the time we entered our thirties, faith didn't feel very faithful to us. Where we went from that point obviously differed, but I could certainly understand him. Real climbers know how close we are from jumping off all the time.

Every day, we are somewhere between giving up and going harder than ever.

Both of our individual relationships with God were shaped primarily by the climb. Even though our mountains were noble, effective, and called "ministry," my friend and I didn't always keep God close as we climbed. A good, sound, developed, and often revisited "why"—the reason we climb—is necessary on your journey up. We all take a bag of that reason up the mountain, but as we climb, our "why" tends to get squeezed out by accumulated comparisons, accolades, applause, responsibilities, and ego. That potent, meaningful, innocent "why" is dropped and left to roll back down, leaving us with no other sustenance than how loudly the crowd screams, how much our children succeed and credit us, or how often we get promoted.

The mountain doesn't have much for us to eat, but it seems like it feeds on our blood, sweat, and tears; our faith; our resolve; and the inner child that just wants to be with and approved by "Dad."

Maybe all of us are called to climb at least one mountain in this life, but I don't believe the mountain is where we're meant to live out all the days of our lives. It took some scrapes, loneliness, and intense conversations in the thin air to realize that what I needed, perhaps I once had. And I certainly could have again.

In the valley.

CHAPTER 3

DISCOVER THE VALLEY

I had a feeling my grandmother would die on Christmas.

Her three-year descent into dementia seemed to have hit rock bottom. She was no longer eating. No longer talking. Barely staying asleep. Barely staying awake. It had been this way for weeks now, even through her ninety-eighth birthday. I knew this queen could never go out on a *regular* day. If not Thanksgiving, then her birthday. And if not her birthday, then Christmas.

But also, if I make it all about me—which a lot of us do when it comes to the loss of a loved one—after my stoup-triggered tantrum earlier that December, I felt like at least one more punch in the stomach was coming.

My share of great phone calls has always come in the morning. My whole career started with a morning call. At the beginning of my climb—I was barely legal, near the end of college—I would wake up and check my phone, anticipating great announcements, updates, and moves of God in my life. But after a while, I'd wake up every day and hurriedly check my phone to make sure the sky hadn't fallen.

And on this Christmas Day, the sky had fallen a little bit.

An odd mix of sadness and relief sat on my shoulders. In a way, I had mourned her death months before she died. The grandmother I knew—the funny, spunky, salmon-croquette-cooking, large-font-Bible-reading lady who always sat in that one brick-red recliner—had been lost years before she left this earth.

I rolled out of the stiffly made hotel bed, three years and a mile away from my last Chicago home. Ten years and twenty miles from that brick-red chair. I grabbed my Santa-esque sack of presents for the family and walked to the car. Picking up my mother, I headed to my aunt's house, where my grandmother had been living for the past couple of years, and solemnly walked up the stairs. We apparently just missed the funeral-home reps removing the body from her room.

As the house filled up, the atmosphere was strangely OK. There were way more off-topic jokes than on-topic tears. While her last moments and words were retold several times throughout the day, there was a peacefulness about Grandma's life and death that encouraged us to get along with celebrating Christmas.

No one really cried.

Until I did.

But it wasn't because of Grandma.

Sydney, my brilliant first cousin, with the memory of an elephant, was kicking a path through the chaos of gift boxes in front of the tree. We don't hang out as much as adults, but we regularly recall our golden summers when we could watch *Home Alone 2* and *Gilligan's Island* all day. From summer camp to Disney World to her racist grandparents' house downstate, we were joined at the hip. And of all the family members who could have been weeping in the corner, Sydney was the one taking care of Grandma in her last days. She was also the one to discover Grandma's lifeless body.

I hadn't even had a chance to ask her how she was feeling, but, committed to the spirit of the holiday, Syd slid a large, unwrapped box over to me. In her typical stone-faced way, she said, "Here, Jonny."

As I keyed through the shipping tape, her contrastingly boisterous mom announced loudly, "She was on eBay and Amazon for weeks looking for that stuff!" I laughed as I wrestled the lid open.

In the box was a vintage water gun, a couple of old action figures, a few toy cars, a game console, and a couple of VHS tapes.

Let me be more specific.

There was a Super Soaker CPS 1200, for constant water pressure on my enemies.

There was a black-and-red Power Ranger action figure. Posable. And ready . . . for my enemies.

Two vintage Hot Wheels cars. That reddish, burgundy-ish Mustang and that black Cougar. So I could outrun my enemies.

A *real* Super Nintendo with cords that probably didn't even fit modern TVs.

And not just any VHS tapes. Don't judge me: *Bibleman* and *Matilda*!

Sydney remembered all the toys I used to play with and love when we were young and, just as her mom broadcasted, she had spent weeks online looking for their exact matches. Unbeknownst to anyone in that house, her gift to me was more than a box of nostalgia. It was a Valley Starter Kit.

My cousin didn't know how bad I was feeling. She didn't know that I had gotten so beholden to the mountain I had become isolated, hungry, and paranoid. She didn't know that just a week prior, I was screaming over minced carrots and stew and canceling shows and film opportunities so I could parachute off this godforsaken mountain. She didn't know that all the achievement and accolades I had been receiving were starting to feel empty and fake. She didn't know I had just signed the deal to write this book. She didn't know how this adult Jonathan felt like everything *but* a son of God.

Sydney's Valley Starter Kit was an invitation for me to be a kid again. But there was a deeper purpose at play. Staring at the box filled with the reminiscences of childhood, I cried. I felt seen. But I also felt a little shame because, at that moment, I finally heard what my ears had been shut off to. I heard God invite me to be a son again.

The Valley Gets Really Bad Press

Remember that music video shoot I shared in the last chapter? I got so into my boy band–rock star fantasy that I risked confusing innocent, impressionable Christians around the world by pointing at the camera and not up "to heaven." I could have been permanently exiled to R&B for that error. According to the eleventh commandment, to refer to God, *you must gesture up.* (Again, joking.) I'm not sure who started it, but the world has generally followed this trend. It was demonstrated early in human history as the Babylonians conspired to build "a tower that reache[d] to the heavens, so that [they could] make a name for [themselves]" (Genesis 11:4). We associate "up" with the divine, the great and powerful.

But now imagine if I had pointed *down.* My Christian fans wouldn't have just been confused but enraged. *All* the music communities would've looked at me strangely. The only direction we have branded as much as up is down.

Down seems to always signify death, evil, Satan, poverty, sadness, failure, and everything hot and terrible. No one wants to go down. No one wants to be lowly and mediocre and sad. The same way mountains are glorified because of their upward construction, valleys, even in our beautiful Bible, are demonized because of their downward composition in comparison.

I mean, just look at how the Bible blasts bad press about the valley!

In Psalm 84, the Sons of Korah—basically a rock-star songwriting group in Israel—wrote a song for the highs and lows of life. The psalm sings that God's presence and love is like a dwelling place. "Even the sparrow has found a home . . . near [God's] altar" (verse 3). God's restoring presence and the strength we can derive from it redeems an otherwise woeful valley. "As they pass through the Valley of Baka, they make it a place of springs; the autumn rains also cover it with pools [blessings]" (verse 6). The Valley of Baka literally means the Valley of Weeping. The valley, here, is presented as a place of despair to be overcome and converted. Sad valley. Bad press.

Here's another one. Ezekiel prophesied over a valley of dry bones in Ezekiel 37. Think about that for a minute. Better yet, picture it. Barren wilderness as far as the eye can see. Dirt, cracked and parched, barely visible underneath a sea of sun-bleached, shattered skeletons. Heaps of leg bones, ribs, and skulls litter the dust. Desolate. It's a depressing scene. God commanded Ezekiel to speak life into the skeletons and watch how breath and movement would be restored to the lifeless bones. God used this demonstration to symbolize the awakening and the reestablishing of Israel. And he did it with these dry, lifeless bones found where? A dry valley. *More* bad press.

Need another example? I got you. Psalm 23:4 is the most popular valley reference there is, and, of course, it's bringing the death vibes. "Even though I walk through the valley of the shadow of death, I fear no evil, for You are with me" (NASB). No, David! Not you too! There wasn't a literal "valley of the shadow of death," but David's poetry used the valley as, once again, a symbol of danger, darkness, and concern. Therefore, for the valley, even more bad press. The valley is normally described as a place you absolutely don't want to be.

A sad valley. A dry valley. A dark valley. This is what we now expect of valleys!

I'm from Chicago. We don't have mountains or valleys. We have one hill around 111th Street and a few mountains of garbage and grass at the city dump. And they stink—literally. So, thanks to Sunday church characterizing the valley as miserable and without much personal observation, I imagined valleys were the scary armpits between mountains probably five hundred feet below sea level, twenty feet above hell.

My second home in LA, though? Well, there are *plenty* of peaks and valleys there. In fact, it's full of communities characterized by and named after their topography. Think "The Hills," neighborhoods in the Santa Monica Mountains that reek of affluence and success.

And then there's "The Valley," the suburbanized San Fernando Valley, where you get more bang for your buck thanks to its absence of drip . . . and height. Unlike The Hills, The Valley, particularly the lowest parts of it, is generally unremarkable.

Years before I moved to LA, when I had my first show there, I remember feeling bad for everyone who told me they lived in The Valley. I imagined the infamous 405 Freeway sunk down ten thousand feet, and there a couple million sad humans questioned why they'd moved West in the first place. (I won't take the opportunity to make the easy, broken-Hollywood-dream joke here.)

I had grown up on flat land, so I remember sitting in the back of a black SUV going down that highway and experiencing that first descent down a hill. It seemed huge then. Once I moved there, I never could find that precipitous drop I remembered, but I did come face-to-face with the "order of elevation" that gives social structure to the City of Angels. With some exceptions, the higher on the hill you live, the richer you are.

And my house was in a canyon—a narrow valley created by a river. By LA standards, this meant I was not extremely wealthy or living way beyond my means, for the houses on the bottom of the mountain are normally more modest and unimpressive. Every day, as I approached my West Hollywood home, though, I saw this particular huge white house on the top of one of the mountains. I have been told several unverified stories of who may live there, but all I really know is, whoever they are, they've got money—and lots of it.

Throughout Los Angeles, and around the world, there are neighborhoods of extreme beauty and wealth that exist off the mountain and in lower-lying areas. But that doesn't seem to take away from the mystique of living *above* people and building a residence on the mountain.

The mountain has such *good* publicity, with its potential riches, fame, accolades, and glory, that people who haven't even started climbing yet can't wait to get to the top. But since the valley has historically come with such *negative* connotations, it is much more difficult to convince a climber to come back down. Stress, anxiety, and pressure gnaw at the bones of a climber. Isolation, lack of spiritual sustenance, and the fear of falling choke the life out of climbers every day. Still, for many of us, that agony beats pausing, simplifying, and living outside of the grind, even for an hour, a day, or a season.

Can the artist turn down the gig?

Can the executive trust someone else to take the reins for a while?

Can the entrepreneur consider something other than the growth of their business?

Stripping off your titles or forsaking the grind and spending time in the valley may sound scary, counterproductive, or even like you're admitting defeat. But the way I see it, the valley has everything the climber's soul has been longing for. Everything the climber deserves. Everything the mountain doesn't have.

A New Way to Look at the Valley

The poetry and symbolism of the Bible, and even of many cultures outside of Judeo-Christianity, cast God in the clouds, so the valleys, especially when compared to high mountains, seem dangerously far away from Him and His symbolically airborne residence. Biblical poetry casts valleys as the deadly places, when the most dangerous valley in the world has a mortality rate of 0.00034 percent.[1] The most dangerous mountain? Thirty-two percent.[2] Contrary to all the poetry, the valley, most of the time, is not some walkway through hell but a place of fertility, beauty, and nourishment. The mountains look amazing in the distance, but there's a reason the cradle of civilization originated in the valley regions.

The valley provides what the mountain doesn't.

This valley that I write about, of course, is not geographical. I can't point you east or west to this great oasis that will work for your renewal. It is no more tangible than the mountain you spend every day trying to climb.

Like the mountain, the valley is a mindset. The valley is not about finishing anything, studying anything, or *doing* anything, but simply *being* a child of God. In this valley, there is shedding of trauma, renewing of identity, a humbling, a de-stressing, and a river of God's recharging presence. The valley may not immediately or profoundly answer whether you should complete that business merger, collaborate with this shady producer, or expand from one Sunday service to three. (It might, though.) The valley is for the climber's health. The valley feeds the *human* and their soul. And here is why we can't survive the mountain without it.

For one, the rigors of the mountain don't allow for much intimacy. When you are climbing—and therefore operating at the fringes of your ability—there is less time to exchange fears, wisdom, joys, and sorrows. A life spent accomplishing leaves little room for intimate conversations. Excessive time in the studio means less energy for friends and relational nourishment. A forced people-pleasing smile masks deep fatigue and lack.

From my experience, a single person climbing their mountain may find it easier to engage in a temporary *form* of intimacy—particularly physical, ahem . . . sexual. Rather than curing each other's loneliness, we are just lonely *together*. And that slice of tenderness on an otherwise lonely mountain can build intense bonds that come with the sound of a Ferrari but have the power of a golf cart. The reckoning usually comes when the health of the relationship demands deprioritizing the climb. It is incredible how much the mountain mindset rooted in career, purpose, and assignment frames every decision we make, even in other spheres of life.

For years, the only consistent and convenient intimacy I could get while climbing—recording, traveling, touring, winning, losing, and struggling to maintain an "acceptable" public image—were the women I tried to vet, enjoy, indulge in, and resist. All at the same time.

As I mentioned earlier, the mountain has a way of revealing and intensifying the cracks in your foundation. So, when your weakness is the opposite sex, there are always love interests—which can morph into heavy burdens—that you will desperately attempt to carry up the mountain with you. I recognized this injurious pattern in my life when I reengaged with my valley. Or, rather, when God ushered me down to my valley, and suddenly I was surrounded by *male* friends, peers, and elders who understood what the climb could do to a young man. It wasn't strictly women, or physical intimacy, I needed. It was also friendship and mentorship, the honest kind, that could relate to my weakness and address my truest needs. And that could only be found when I wasn't working, competing, and grinding. It could only be found when I stopped to consider the climber, the son underneath.

Men aren't always the best at this, but off the mountain, my friends and I found space to be vulnerable. Most men are encouraged to climb multiple mountains in their lifetime, and often our conversations reflect the competitiveness, numbness, and objectivity required to live in that rarefied air. But in the valley, I was able to cultivate some conversations by being honest and open about what life was doing to me. Adults in general, but certainly men in the many communities I have traversed, are struggling to various extents with the pressure of performance, the pressure of choice, and the pressure of the climb. In secret, we figured we were the only ones not finding happiness on the rocky slopes. In secret, we figured we were the only ones not even sure the mountain we'd chosen to climb was the right one to begin with. In secret, we figured we were the only ones tired of operating at the fringes of our abilities just to find and cement our place in society.

While I was steeped in the mountain mindset, I stretched to make time for female relationships only because of the dependable and steady benefits—and hope—they offered.

Those queens were attracted to my *mettle* on the rough slopes, the *medals* I had earned on the way up, and the *metal* crown promised at the end of the road. But I never gave myself enough time alone—without them and without my work—to find the iron that would sharpen my iron. During the climb, there is only time to soothe and wrap the wounds—the letdowns, the hurts, the disappointments accumulated along the journey—so you can continue upward and not leave behind a trail of blood on the way. And that's what some relationships do—soothe and wrap. Let's just say, I did not lack in those types of relationships. The valley is beautifully distinct, though, as it's there that God provides a different, healthy type of healing, community, and intimacy, often through people during intentional, focused time away from the grind.

The second beautiful distinction between the mountain and the valley are the resources the valley provides for abundant living. Along the Nile, the Tigris, and the Mississippi River valleys, people from early civilizations could find fertile soil, reliable access to water, fishing, and ease of transportation. No matter how rugged, remote, or snowcapped the mountain, the valley is often lush green. Nutrition and sustenance are not difficult to find. Despite the poetry, even biblical poetry that would convey otherwise, the valley is normally bustling with life because it is bustling with the elements that give life!

The mountain's scarcity presents itself as a lack of time for Sunday sermons and deep conversation. There isn't time to sit in the presence of loving prophets and teachers. There isn't enough available energy to seek out good nutrition for the soul. There isn't time to enjoy divinely, carefully prepared meals. No, on the mountain we are running on dirty Chai lattes with a double espresso shot.

The valley provides the life-giving words, the faith-fortifying conversations, and the mind-changing moments that can only be discovered in God's presence. Sound theology lets us know that God is always with us and we will never leave His presence, even on the mountain. David opined of the Lord in Psalm 139:8, "If I go up to the heavens, you are there; if I make my bed in the depths, you are there."

The valley mindset, however, is the venue where we can be *aware* of that presence—and respond.

Third, unlike the mountain, the land in the valley is more easily navigable and forgiving. So much of the mountain experience is worrying about how not to fall. It's hard to fall to your death when you're already on the ground. I suppose you could twist an ankle or something, but your likelihood of making a fatal mistake is much lower when you're in the valley.

As a gospel artist, there are musical ways to alienate your audience, business ways to tank your career, ethical ways to lose people, and moral ways to lose value. And the higher those pressures pushed me up the mountain, the more I feared falling right off.

Too much of my time, energy, and bandwidth was being used up, wondering how to avoid falling.

How to avoid making mistakes.

How to avoid keeping my mistakes from ruining my life.

The valley is a safe place. The valley is full of grace. The valley wants you to confess so you don't carry fear, condemnation, and faithlessness throughout your assignment. The valley gives all "who are weary and burdened . . . rest" (Matthew 11:28).

> The valley wants you to confess so you don't carry fear, condemnation, and faithlessness throughout your assignment.

There's a reason people live in the valleys. They can actually *live* there.

Maybe they aren't climbing new heights at that moment, braving harsh temperatures and thin air, but they are alive! The valley offers fuel for life—intimacy, nutrition, and peace of mind. Without too much special technology, anatomical evolution, or fuss, the valley—*your* valley—has what it takes for you to live that "abundant life" promised in John 10:10.

The Benefits of Being on the Ground

If the mountain represents your pursuit and progress in your chosen career, calling, assignment, or purpose, the valley represents the place—the mindset—where that achievement and upward progress is not necessary.

The mountain offers titles like CEO, star, manager, graduate, specialist, but the valley only has use of "son" or "daughter." The valley is the psychological venue for the reconnection with God and the part of you that does not need to accomplish, win, pursue, progress, or compete. In nature, the valley is normally a place of life, nourishment, and vibrance. A valley mindset shares the same traits and, therefore, denotes a place of rest, recovery, refilling, retooling, refreshment, and repurposing. In other words, the valley gives you exactly what you need.

When is the last time you thought about what you need? Think about it. Beyond money for bills, a new strategy for crypto, or another big break, what do *you* really need? So much of God's messaging in the Bible is aimed at the soul of a human being, despite the financial, social, and even medical condition of that human being. It often is the persecuted, the poor, the mourning, and the meek who are woefully acquainted with what they need as *humans*, unclouded by what they may need as climbers.

Throughout the Bible, it took people being slammed to the ground and blinded by great lights for them to stop climbing, humble themselves, and listen. In the book of Acts, Saul's work was of great renown and reputation. He had climbed the ranks of local religion and piety, but his soul needed work. There was an unrest, a thorn, a shame, even, that could've been fueling his maniacal, violent, and ungodly climb up the mountain. As he traveled to Damascus to continue it, he was stunned by a bright light from heaven and fell to the ground, potentially falling off his horse. When he got up from the ground, Saul could no longer see. He was blind for three days, and God's answer to healing his blindness was Ananias, a follower of Christ, whom Saul was likely coming to persecute. Ananias, reluctant at first for good reason, prayed for Saul, and Saul was healed. Off the mountain but healed. The valley—which he was knocked down into—saved him and gave him the purpose, the revelation, and the community he needed.[3]

Our prayers on the mountain generally concern the mountain, the protection of progress, and the strength to conquer the next obstacle. Prayers in the valley are based around simply being closer to God and reposing in His fatherly embrace.

Our thoughts on the mountain are of productivity, results, opportunities, and threats. In the valley our thoughts can stay on "whatever is true, whatever is noble, whatever is right, whatever is pure, whatever is lovely, [and] whatever is admirable" (Philippians 4:8).

Our conversations on the mountain are for information, insight, networking, and advantage. Our conversations in the valley are for enjoyment, restoration, curiosity, and intimacy.

The valley represents life *near* our mountains, but not *on* them. The shadow that your big mountain may cast over your life does not have to prevent you from spending time in the valley. Your church still needs you. Your career is still moving. Your fans are still anticipating. Your children are still making requests. Yes, the mountain is *near*, and maybe it will always be, but you can still operate for a moment, a day, or a season off it—in the valley.

Can you remember an era where your mind wasn't preoccupied with climbing but rather just frolicking at the bottom of the mountain? Before the Grammys, before tours, before millions of followers, and before Instagram, I lived gleefully in the valley. My little hills were grades, basketball games, and test scores. But I didn't need to be better than anyone. I wasn't interested in taking on the highest mountains. I wanted to have fun and learn the new Chicago Mass Choir song on the organ. Even as I became a young adult, I could walk into church and cry if I wanted, dance if I wanted, grab extra candy from the pastor's office and argue with the church secretary about it if I wanted. (Pastor Jackson gave me permission *carte blanche* as far as the candy was concerned.) This valley wasn't set up for me to break any glass ceilings or make my mark on the world in any extraordinary way; it was set up for me to live.

Our culture is not concerned with us living, though. No, our culture encourages us to grind, hustle, party, and die young. It challenges us to lead a short life characterized by notches on belts, the pursuit of viral moments, cool-looking backdrops to post online, and a very shallow clout, best acquired by quick, cocaine-fueled sprints up the mountain. So the idea of a valley—whether it's the one from childhood, or one of stillness and prayer, or one of Sabbath rest and fun—is unnatural to our modern brains, unappealing to minds hardwired to impress and experience God's favor *only* in enlarged and rising territory.

Throughout my life, the most visible evidence of God's blessing and presence—to me—had always been the way he protected and bolstered my career. I have taught—and am still teaching—myself to recognize the overriding peace, the protection of my heart, the access to love and revelation, and my status as his son as evidence too. I must admit, through the first decade or so of adulthood, creating ways for me to safely climb higher and finding miraculous footholds that kept me from falling lower was all I prayed about and appreciated God for. Prayers for the enlargement of territory, the heightening of my platform, and the preservation of my name fit more comfortably in my culture's "rise and grind" theme. As I get a little older, I see that broadening my reach is nowhere near as important as broadening my vision, and neither are as sufficient for life as broadening my peace and joy.

> Broadening my reach is nowhere near as important as broadening my vision.

Closer, but Not Quite the Valley

I've told you a lot about the beginning of my climb and how things have been going lately. Storybook start, followed by big tours and Grammys. But perhaps I've left out a bit of the middle.

From 2013 to, let's say, 2018, after every show, pouring my heart out, sweating, and feeling incredibly self-conscious and vulnerable, I had to play politics and smile for a seemingly never-ending trickle of "VIPs"—the pastors, and the pastors' daughters, who supposedly had a crush on me. Then

I'd keep up the good spirits for the potentially unprofessional or nosy escort and chauffeur as we'd drive away. And then I'd get to a hotel room, apart from any crew or friends or bandmates, and figure out how to recover alone. Half the time, we got to the hotel too late for room service. And if there *was* food, it wasn't good food. And if there was good food, I guarantee it was not healthy food. I'd try, normally unsuccessfully, to fall asleep quickly on all the adrenaline, as the promoter typically bought the cheapest flight, usually leaving at 6:00 a.m., which meant I needed to be at the airport by 5:00 a.m. The airport would be at least forty minutes away, so lobby call would be at 4:15 a.m. And I really didn't have the energy to shower or pack the night before, so my alarm would go off at 3:45 a.m.—and the day would begin.

Glory to God for how many people were aware of me, my music, and my face back then. And at the airport, on three hours of broken sleep, I'd try my best to maintain a smile for gospel-loving TSA agents and my fellow passengers who needed me to stand still for a few moments while they figured out where they knew me from. As we'd take off toward the sky, the sun, having completed its glorious entrance into the day, would beam at my face through the window of the one passenger who wanted to read, thus keeping me awake to face another eighteen hours without rest.

The plane life is for the birds—literally. Only the birds should be up there that much!

But then one day, in 2019, I was introduced to the bus tour.

From bus/bed, to stage, and back to the bus. From spotlighted edge of the mountain to a cave of slight rest, in three hundred feet—thirty seconds if I really ran for it.

Bussing around a gospel artist to clubs, theaters, and everything but churches was rare and untested. Up to this point, our only outlet was to travel from church to church, singing for the old, the young, the new converts, and the veterans all at the same time. But now I got to sing to a room of just *my* fans. The specific people I caught in those wide Sunday nets now came together, like-minded in love for my music.

But most of all: no TSA.

Every year since 2019, the bulk of my touring life has been carried out in an organized, themed bus tour. Better, longer, more fun shows that were an expression of my art. And with that mobile, restful cave close by.

As soon as that heavy aluminum door shut, I no longer needed to keep up any airs, any image, any work ethic, any pursuit. I'd hold my breath as I flipped through the Instagram stories and the clips from the show that fans had posted. The big mistakes, the bad notes, the time I almost tripped, the forgotten words, and the lighting and sound miscues weren't so bad from their perspective. Instead, I heard them singing louder than my missed notes. I saw them connecting with God's work through me more than my own work, my own performance. And honestly, I saw myself, a little bit more, as a product of God's grace, an extension of his legacy, a son, through their cameras.

After I caught my breath, I'd begin to take off the tour outfit, take off the day, and take off the responsibility. That "woosah" was normally interrupted within minutes, though, as I'd hear the audience beginning to pour out of the venue and walk past our bus lot, lingering with their friends and searching for their cars.

I couldn't help but listen for their appraisal of the night. So I'd keep the day, the outfit, and the responsibility on a little while longer.

I didn't revel in the job well done—the climb well done. I didn't consider what God could have been saying *to* me inside the success and hype. Instead, I'd think of ways for the next show to be better and how to include some of the songs they'd apparently wished I'd sung. I let just enough sunlight in to temporarily warm up the side of the cold cliff, to make the mountain feel OK. Unfortunately, that little bit of rest and satisfaction on the mountain convinced me I didn't need to go further down into God's arms. I wish I had gone all the way down, though. Perhaps I would have internalized something lasting and let this successful moment confirm God's identity in me and His love for me. But no, I let the sun give me just enough warmth to keep climbing again.

During the time I was writing this book, I was standing in a hotel elevator alone one night, desperately patting and probing my pockets for a single key card. Some hotels don't allow you to press your floor number until you have successfully scanned your key card, and this was one of them. Well, I guess I took forever to find it, because the closed doors jolted open again and an unassuming young lady, around thirty, giggled as she walked in. She had a big hiking back-pack, and since my mind had been so attuned to mountains and mountain climbers, I had to ask, "Why do you have *that* kind of backpack on?" It just didn't fit this business class hotel in Chicago, a land of very little hikeable terrain. She laughed and said she'd just gotten back from climbing Cerro Aconcagua, the tallest mountain in the Western Hemisphere, on the border of Argentina and Chile. How serendipitous was that? I asked her if she'd be open to having a conversa-tion about her adventures, and she sweetly obliged.

This climber, April Martinez, and I talked for nearly an hour, and I watched her affable San Diegan smile give way to deeper, maybe even darker, thoughts. At a remarkably young age, she could already say she was a military vet and an accomplished mountaineer. I prodded past her initial com-mercial of how climbing widens her idea of what adversity she can handle and complete. She revealed that a very important skill on the mountain is, in essence, being able to forget your last success and failure so that your next steps are not com-promised. Perhaps it is often beneficial to compartmentalize some bad experiences, but the mountain mindset doesn't automatically shift when the experiences are good. April admitted that the rhythm she'd learned from countless days on the mountain had a deleterious effect on her happiness, as "you don't know how to sit with all that you've done."

The mountain has its moments. God does build in chances for us to feel good, accomplished, and significant on the mountain. But the true value of accomplishment is reduced and fleeting without time spent in the valley to explore its worth. Simply put, achievement doesn't feel as good, doesn't build you up as well, until you share it with the Father and the folks who loved you without it. No matter how fulfilling some mountain moments—great feedback, followers, accolades, promotions, high-productivity weeks—may be, I've noticed that the mountain only allows you to be *on* it. It is not built to house you, keep you, or love you back.

The valley, however, with all its green and genial grace, gives you room to be *in* it. It is the setting where we can be with ourselves and God and marinate in His benefits.

Admission to the upper echelons of the mountain requires titles, accolades, and higher responsibility. It requires addition.

Admission to the valley requires stripping those titles off—subtraction. It's a space with God reserved for you *minus* all the extra glory, caution, or things to consider. It may feel impossible to climb down and detach yourself from the added pressure and platform. But you can do it. And your life will be changed once you know how to work on the mountain but *live* in the valley.

Four years into my bus tour era, only months removed from that December collapse, I still didn't know how to get back down to the valley, but my tour bus—my RV—gave me some early glimpses of what that valley could be.

I still had a way to go. I'd left my Valley Starter Kit at home, and my RV had no VHS player. So, no *Matilda*. Not yet, at least.

CHAPTER 4

REMEMBER WHO YOU ARE

I think I've figured out why moms are so frustratingly "momm-y."

Let me preface my upcoming remarks by saying I love my mother. As a matter of fact, that's what makes this phenomenon so interesting to me. I mean, I love her to death! The thought of her smile, her sacrifice, and her contentment in this season of life often overwhelms me with joy and gratitude. I miss her all the time, and I'm not too grown up to admit that sometimes a cry on her shoulder still makes me feel better. Oh, how I love Janis.

Sometimes I want to hear her voice and make sure she's OK—and honestly make sure I'm OK, because, of course, moms always know.

But once she answers my phone call and begins her survey of my head and heart, I've noticed how quickly I lose patience.

I know I'm not the only adult who rapidly loses serenity when talking to their mom. No matter how much you feel like you've got things under control and are moving at a good pace, moms always seem to be a bit incompatible with that rhythm.

I may have spent the last hours, days, and weeks climbing successfully and intensely up my mountain. But Mom doesn't know that. She is not aware of the recording sessions, boardroom meetings, social conquests, and Instagram praise. And even if she were, my mother is not compelled to relate to the mountain version of me. She does not see a CEO, an award winner, or even a dutiful king. She sees her son. And probably just an overgrown version of her month-old baby.

Outside of her and a few aunts and godmothers, everyone else on the planet tends to treat me based on my elevation, my career, and my status in life. Society is like that in general. People tend to relate to other people based on their post. Pastor. Boss. Employee. Legend. President. Peasant. *Moms*, however, generally connect their adult kids to the babies they once nursed. In that sense, moms aren't always the best at giving advice on mountain issues. They may not understand how your industry works, the content of the contract, or the public's response. Though I may need counsel on how to reach the next rock, my mom can't always offer that. This is because, for the most part, moms specialize in valley talk. A recent conversation my mom and I had speaks for itself.

I hadn't been awake for long, but after a quick prayer, a quick read of missed texts, and a quick scroll on Instagram,

I had three things on my mind: this book, the new label I'd founded, and the fact that I hadn't checked on my mom in a couple of days. So I ran into my studio, woke up my laptop, and put Microsoft Word on one side of the screen and Pro Tools, the recording software, on the other. I played my recent recording session in the background as I dumped a few stream-of-consciousness paragraphs on chapter 3, to make sense of later.

Five minutes in—before I could forget again—I video-called my mom.

"Hey, Ma."

"Hey, kiddo!"

Holding back slight tears at the sight of her face I so dearly missed, I still tried to make it clear I wasn't going to be on the phone for long. "Just thinking about you. Checking on you."

She was relaxed, happy to see me. She also *dragged* out every sentence she spoke. Every period equaled three excruciating seconds. "I'm good." *Three second pause.* "Where are you?"

"I'm home."

"You don't look like you're at home. What room is that?"

"The studio."

"Oh, it doesn't look familiar. When did you get back?"

"Yesterday."

"Oh, OK." *Three, two, one.* "How are you feeling?"

(I *felt* the mountain climber inside starting to do cartwheels in my head.) Sighing, I responded, "I'm good, how are you?"

"Oh, I'm good. Just took a walk over to the office." Retired from over forty years of administrative assistance, she couldn't seem to actually retire. "Did you know they built a new church on that lot around the corner?"

"No, no I didn't, Ma."

"Hmmm, I figured you might know about it." When I showed no interest or insight on this particular topic, she shifted the conversation to my babysitter from preschool. "Have you talked to Mama Janet lately?"

"No, is she OK?"

"She's fine. I just bet she'd like to hear from you."

My lungs choked at the thought of *even more* time off the mountain to talk to another wonderful old lady. "Uhhh . . . yeah . . . OK, Mom. I will."

"Hmmm." *Three, two, one.* "When are the Grammys?"

"Like February, Ma." (It was currently November.)

"Are you going?"

"I guess so. That's far away, though. But anyway . . ."

I knew she could sense my dismount. "Oh . . . OK." *Three, two, one.* "I was talking to Sis Berdell the other day, and she was just going on and on about you. Actually, a lot of people come up to me saying they are praying for you. You should give her a call."

Another wonderful old lady to call? Yikes. "Umm . . . OK, when I get a chance, but anyway, I just called . . ."

"Yes, you are so loved. I was listening to your album today. It's really the best one in your category. You just have such good words."

"Thanks, Ma, but you know, all awards are uphill battles."

"I know, but it's so good." *Three, two, one.* "What are you doing tomorrow?"

"Just doing some more work. Matter fact, I should probably get to . . ."

"OK. When are you coming to Chicago?"

"No time soon, I don't think. But let me, uh . . ."

"Don't rush me. How's [any random person I knew a hundred years ago but haven't seen since]?"

Valley talk. Five minutes of straight valley talk. Her words, even her questions, weren't career- or climb-centered. Her perspective, as always, soul-, life-, and love-centered. "How are you feeling?" "Where are you?" "You are so loved." I may not have allowed her much time to fully articulate herself, but if you paid attention to the few words she *could* get out, you'll notice she was telling me, "People are in your corner," "With or without awards, your work is good," and "You have lots to look forward to."

Valley talk! Her verbal expressions weren't especially profound or poetic. My mom wasn't *trying* to be uplifting, encouraging, or impactful. She was just talking to and caring for her son. Without trying, her words were laced with love, affirmation, gentle reminders, refocusing, and self-assessment.

And I waved each sentence away like a pesky fly.

I've realized that the more preoccupied I am with the mountain, the more my mom's "momm-ing"—her slow, steady, unconditional love—gets on my nerves. And before I know it, as I've noticed in many other conversations I've had with her, I become irritable, rushing through her questions and regretting the precious time I wasted on not climbing. The more I am consumed by achieving, progressing, grinding, maintaining, and *adulting*, the less compatible I become with her motherly pace. The less comfortable I am slowing into the role of "son."

Getting into the valley mindset means returning to your stable identity as a son or daughter of God. Which begs the question: Does our fixation with the mountain speed us up so much that our stride becomes incompatible with God's *fatherly* pace too?

A Child's Power

I grew up in one of the fourteen million families in the US with a single mom.[1] My sister, who was in college by the time I was born, was out of the house most of my childhood, so I was left as mom's lone company. Without a car, our major modes of transportation included the comprehensive Chicago public transit system and the school bus. Living paycheck to paycheck, by the time I was in fifth grade, come blizzard, sickness, half day, missed bus, or any chaos the Southside could present, my mom was *going* to work. Which meant there were times I was left to brave Jeffery Boulevard alone.

What I'm about to say may scare the current generation of micromanager parents who are understandably paranoid about the germy, violent, and conspiracy-theory-ridden world around them. But brace yourselves. Growing up, I experienced so many life-shaping, heart-wrenching, death (or serious injury)-defying moments—all which occurred completely unbeknownst to my mother. I'm talking dicey interactions with gangs, stray dogs, store clerks, and neighborhood bullies that she will never know about. So much drama and lawlessness happened in the two blocks between my house on Eighty-First and the candy store on Seventy-Ninth that I had to—and chose to—assess and manage on my own. My mother was at work, so there was no running home and crying to Mommy.

I was in similar company. In the streets and alleys, the concrete playgrounds and liquor stores (which also sold candy, chips, and juice—relax!), just beyond the watchful eye of our schoolteachers, underneath the radar of the police, and miles away from working moms, a lot of the kids in my community were riled up by the hip-hop culture, the tempting freedom, and the bubbling anger of low-class living and fatherlessness. In the absence of those dads, and sometimes even mothers, the concept of *son* or *daughter* was less fleshed out, less understood, less valued.

Instead, from a very young age, we kids from the Southside, specifically "over East," were taught to rise above childlike dependence and innocence so we could fend for ourselves and fight for our own undeveloped and tenuous honor. Being "grown"—that is, walking around with the swagger, conviction, and audacity we believed adults had to have, before you had any body hair—was a badge of honor. The hood had its own way of draining the child out of childhood.

But as I observe culture, this phenomenon is not only reserved for adolescents from the inner cities. Even children from the suburbs are at risk not only of being stripped of their innocence, but also devaluing that innocent part of life that isn't for human consumption. These days, it seems like as soon as a kid displays any type of precociousness, gift, personality, or confidence, they are given a mountain to climb. They are given a bag to chase. They are given an audience to cater to. Those kids earn heavy titles like "performer," "star," "baller." But sometimes, they also lose the title of "child."

Both the Southside of Chicago back in the 2000s and the overly ambitious culture today cheapen the significance of the titles "son" and "daughter." Often, it's because we connect the words with weakness, dependence, and mediocrity.

To us, "son" or "daughter" is supposed to be a starting place, not a permanent identity. After all, we are no longer children. We've already graduated from being our parents' child a long time ago—like maybe the second we got a car or a dorm room. We are CEOs now, or college grads, or mothers of three. We are grown. Doing things. Capable. Leading other people. We have zero time to be weak, needy, or ordinary.

As you search the Scriptures, though, God places incredible significance on what it means to be His child. He does not call His people "sons" and "daughters" to emphasize our *weaknesses*. And He certainly could because, compared to Him, we are pretty pitiful. "The weakness of God is stronger than human strength" (1 Corinthians 1:25). God doesn't even harp on our *dependence* when He calls us His children. Though every Christian knows we truly are to "lean not on [our] own understanding" but rather "in all [our] ways submit to him" (Proverbs 3:5–6).

Instead, "son" or "daughter" indicated *derived power and privilege*. The moniker was not used to subjugate, but to empower. After John baptized Jesus, the Holy Spirit descended onto Jesus, and immediately afterward, God referred to Jesus as His Son. It was a mark of approval. It was a declaration of imparted strength and status. It was everything a man would want—and Jesus hadn't performed a single miracle yet. God had publicly declared Jesus' identity as His Son, and Jesus hadn't *climbed* an inch!

In American basketball culture, when your opponent completely embarrasses you with a move that shows their superior athleticism or strength, it may be said that you were "sonned." The thought here is that you were outclassed, outmuscled, too weak, too unskilled, and out of your league. Basically, you're just a boy among men. It's fun to say on the court, but this vernacular is certainly not compatible with the Bible's characterization of "son." Sons were empowered like Jesus was. Their paths were defined like Solomon's was.

Their dreams were bigger like Joseph's were. Their impact was multiplied like Elisha's was.

Even in Israel, circa 1400 BCE, a woman's status as a "daughter" could secure her that derived status and privilege. The Bible, in Numbers 27, tells us a story about the daughters of Zelophehad during the time Moses led the people of Israel. Their father had died in the wilderness and, at the time, there was no law by which they, as women, could inherit their deceased father's land. The five daughters approached Moses and bravely requested possession of that land. Moses consulted God, and God told Moses that the daughters should reap Zelophehad's inheritance. This ruling shifted the law in Israel forever. In that culture, *daughter-hood* said they deserved it.

Our perspective on women has changed greatly since then, but more significantly, the Word tells us "[there is no] male and female, for you are all one in Christ Jesus. If you belong to Christ, then you are Abraham's seed, and heirs according to the promise" (Galatians 3:28–29). Basically, what God offers to men in the valley—sonship, power, status, and privilege—is also equally and unequivocally offered to women. Just in case there was any doubt. The valley is for everyone.

Modern culture will try and make you believe sonship or daughterhood are beneath you. As if these positions of weakness should expire when you turn eighteen years old. But God holds them as statures of honor, privilege, progress, and might. Being a son or daughter is more than an ancestral name; it is your divine identity.

Don't let the glorious mountain fool you. The highest position you will ever hold is as a child of God. The grounding we gain in Him is more significant than anything we could ever reach for. The highest place you can ever be is in the valley with Him.

A Child's Right

I remember finally paying attention to the child support checks that were coming to our house around my tenth birthday.

A few months earlier, I had a memorable conversation with that infamous cousin, Sydney, who gives the best Christmas presents. Whenever I'd sleep over at her house, I knew I'd be getting both the top bunk and an earful from her until she fell asleep.

This particular night, I can't remember why, but she asked me, "Where is your father?"

It was a great question. "I don't think I have one," I replied.

"Everybody has one."

"I guess not me."

That may sound like a pretty sad dialogue, but at that point in my life, I felt so sufficiently *uncled* and *godfathered* and *pastored* that I barely noticed the lack of a father in the house. My nerdy brain highlighted this core memory in Jonny history as my first bit of cognitive dissonance, where the truth of my experience and behavior didn't line up with the truth of reason. Intellectually, I knew that along with my mom, I must have had a male parent, too, but at the same time, I couldn't believe what I couldn't see. I knew my answer to Sydney was wrong, but I accepted it anyway. Instead of questioning my experience, I questioned biology.

At the risk of perpetuating a stereotype, I must be true to my experience. Sydney—living in the suburbs—was used to present fathers. I—living in the hood—was not. Not only did I have paternal replacements in my uncles and male family friends, I also did not live in an environment where my fatherlessness would stand out.

That tenth birthday, though, I was a month into attending a new school for fifth grade. It was a school for "high performing" children all around the city, which meant a much more diverse school with many kids who lived a vastly different life.

There were a lot more mansions. A lot more houses on the hill. And a lot more fathers.

For the first time, I felt inferior to my classmates. Not because some were white or wealthy, but because most of them seemed so much more self-assured, cultured, and confident. Up to that point, my schoolmates were mostly concerned with telling "yo mama" jokes and making stupid gestures behind the teachers' backs.

But these *new* kids? They were kicked back. Feet on the desk. Not even just playing Spades, but Bid Whist, a more complicated Spades-like card game that was more popular among Black Baby Boomers than any middle class, mixed-race group of young Millennials. They weren't talking cute crushes and cooties; they were talking long-term girlfriends, triple dates, and spin the bottle. And then at the basketball game, or the bus stop, or at a sleepover, I recognized the biggest difference between me and these kids: a blueprint, a leader, a booster, a provider . . . a father.

Late that fall, as the sun's warmth neglected Chicago once again, my mind went back to those mysterious checks on the coffee table. Maybe my mom had left them there carelessly, assuming my ignorance and disinterest were permanent. Maybe she'd left them there hoping that one day I *would* inquire. Either way, one day, in between Mortal Kombat rounds, I casually walked into the living room and pointed to the top-left corner of the slip of paper and asked, "Is that my dad?"

My mom, watching the evening news on the sofa, was as good at masking her discomfort as any Navy SEAL. I don't even remember if she had fully turned her head toward me when she calmly responded, "Yes. You want to meet him?"

I wasn't ready for a commitment. I was just curious, so I irreverently chimed back, "Not really."

My mom tells me that over the next few days, I didn't lose that nonchalance and apathy toward my dad and the prospect of getting to know him. Back then, I think I was only trying to check a logical box. I was trying to reconcile my experience with the biological fact that *everyone has a father*. I needed visual confirmation that I was not immaculately conceived like Jesus or part of an alien species that had kidnapped my mom. I very noticeably had inherited my face from my mom's side of the family—the McReynoldses. But I needed to see some familiar features in my father's face. Not a full relationship or even a conversation. Just some familiar features.

Unconvinced by my straight face, Mom shared my momentary interest with the guy whose name was on the check. By the end of the week, he and I had talked on the phone. He seemed intelligent and had a "cool cat" rasp and a lisp. Smooth. Genial. What I'd expect out of Smokey Robinson. Nothing wrong with him. And he seemed unfazed by the little energy I returned to him.

A few days after making him pull teeth over the phone, he picked me up from my sister's apartment with a hopeful smile and whisked me away to McDonald's. There was no emotion, no extra joy or catharsis. I remember asking him why I hadn't met him earlier in life. His answer was so vague and impersonal, I chose not to cross-examine him and focused back on my fries.

Something about "[he] and [my] mom's stupidity." Yada, yada, yada.

A couple of unmemorable hours and a Happy Meal later, he dropped me off at home.

My mom asked me if I wanted to continue with the hangouts. And—no surprise here—I again responded, "Not really."

To me, the relationship had already maxed out. I saw a decent man, but I didn't see myself. Perhaps to keep from hurting, I had already built a wall of logical, unemotional processing concerning him. Even the visual confirmation didn't deliver any level of intimacy. And learning *of* him was not the same as learning *from* him.

As the years went by and I experienced my father primarily in the sudden uptick in Christmas and birthday gifts, I started to wonder why it had taken *my* initiation, *my* request, and *my* curiosity to spark our first meeting. He only lived four miles away. And, as I said, there was nothing wrong with him. No drugs, no extra narcissistic vibes, no visible aversion to accountability, and no financial struggles.

Why didn't *he* offer sonship? Why did I have to be the one to ask? I may have checked my own intellectual box, but it gave way to a much more remarkable and unchecked emotional box.

The logical, unemotional way I processed my biological father's absence—and then his sudden but solicited presence—governed how I processed God's availability and willingness to father me. Not feeling worthy of an initiated relationship from my earthly dad made me feel unworthy to be fathered by anyone, including God.

While some of us feel *above* the weak, dependent titles of "son" or "daughter," many of us also feel *beneath* them. We can't accept the concept fully, afraid to seek sonship from God and godly men, because we think that if we deserved it, wouldn't God have provided it already? We unfortunately learn that anything worth having requires greatness, excellence, and achievement of some kind. We stay on the mountain because it offers *earnable,* and therefore understandable and measurable, heights.

The valley, however, is the venue for sonship and daughterhood—*unearned* sonship and daughterhood. And that doesn't come naturally to everyone, particularly the unfathered.

> See what great love the Father has lavished on us, that we should be called children of God! And that is what we are! (1 John 3:1)

Son, take your rightful place. Daughter, claim your spot. It's yours.

A Child's Home

To operate as a boss, a parent, an artist, a principal, a pastor, or as any other role that presents an opportunity to do something and to succeed at it, is to be on the mountain. The mountain is a necessary part of life. We are all expected to work, labor, and accomplish something. We don't reap a harvest without tilling soil, sowing seeds, and caring for the growth.

So how do we connect mountain work with a valley mindset? It's as simple—and as difficult—as working *on* the mountain but living *from* the valley. And we can only make that happen when we operate first and foremost as a son or daughter of God, detached from ambition and accomplishment.

The same way we go to college during the school year but go home for the summer, and the same way we go to our corporate jobs during the day but return home at night, the valley mindset of sonship or daughterhood is your true residence and vantage point.

Remember that as you progress up your mountain, you will eventually notice its scarcity. Over time, as you and everyone around you are working at the fringes of your ability, isolation will kick in and your schedule, your priorities, and your stress may preclude any chances of feeling consistent camaraderie and intimacy. You may also feel as if you're running out of spiritual food up there. You have less time for filling up, reading the Word, and going to church. More time in between you and that last life-changing nugget. Furthermore, the higher you get, guarding against a great fall consumes your mind, taking up more and more space in your strategy, your plans, and the prayers you do get around to praying.

But the venue for sonship and daughterhood—the valley—gives us an opportunity to connect with God and *even people*, apart from work and career. Relating to one another and to God as whole, three-dimensional humans, children, sons, daughters, with fears and beliefs and doubts and quirks, leads to true connection and even friendship. We can't express all these idiosyncrasies on the mountain. If we cry on the mountain, our tears will freeze. But the valley allows you to get weird, and scared, and then recover in God's peaceful presence. What does your current mindset allow you to do?

The Garden of Gethsemane lies at the foot of the Mount of Olives. Recorded in the Gospel of Matthew, we see a version of Jesus in that place that wasn't suitable for immediate public scrutiny and consumption. "'My soul is very sorrowful, even to death; remain here, and watch with me.' And going a little farther he fell on his face and prayed, saying, 'My Father, if it be possible, let this cup pass from me; nevertheless, not as I will, but as you will'" (Matthew 26:38–39 ESV).

Jesus did not exhibit the same swagger in this valley with God that He had on the Mount of Olives. When He was teaching, Pharisees clutched their pearls and laymen fell, enamored with Jesus' audacious and resolute tone. But in the Garden of Gethsemane, He wept, making sure His Father didn't have a less painful plan B for the redemption of the world.

The New Testament writer Luke, describing the same story, said that angels came to strengthen Jesus as He wept. That kind of expression and aid happens in the valley when we truly submit and lean into God as our Father, the sovereign King who is pulling the strings.

In the valley, we speak to God like He can handle anything.

In the valley, we speak to Him like He knows everything.

In the valley, we get what we need because we can admit we have nothing.

If Jesus found space and time to be both human and God, both Son and Savior, certainly we can embrace our own humanity and identities as sons and daughters. In one fell swoop, the valley—the God in the valley—can cure the loneliness, feed the hunger, and give us flatter, lower, safer ground to be ourselves.

A Child's Place

Salvation is offered to the world. It's offered to kings and queens, Black people and white people, bosses and employees, men and women, mothers and fathers. You can walk into church and up to the altar as a beggar or as a seven-figure real estate mogul, as a rising superstar or as a small bodega cashier. There is no one on the planet, regardless of their station in life or level of success, who is left uncovered from God's blanket offer of salvation. God "desires all men to be saved and to come to the knowledge of the truth" (1 Timothy 2:4 NASB1995). All are welcome. But to follow Christ, to receive what is meant *for* the saved, and to enjoy God's promises, you must first and foremost identify as a son or daughter of God.

Jesus taught this lesson often throughout His earthly ministry.

Just then a man came up to Jesus and asked, "Teacher, what good thing must I do to get eternal life?" "Why do you ask me about what is good?" Jesus replied. "There is only One who is good. If you want to enter life, keep the commandments." [. . .] "All these I have kept," the young man said. "What do I still lack?" Jesus answered, "If you want to be perfect, go, sell your possessions and give to the poor, and you will have treasure in heaven. Then come, follow me." When the young man heard this, he went away sad, because he had great wealth. Then Jesus said to his disciples, "Truly I tell you, it is hard for someone who is rich to enter the kingdom of heaven. Again I tell you, it is easier for a camel to go through the eye of a needle than for someone who is rich to enter the kingdom of God." (Matthew 19:16–17, 20–24)

This wealthy young man burst onto the scene before Jesus' death and resurrection. (Obviously, because he's totally talking to Jesus here.) We can only hope that he revisited the idea of following Jesus after learning of the resurrection. At this point in Jewish history, the prevailing thought was that you must *earn* eternal life. By endeavoring to do everything right, you could accomplish salvation. That is a concept the young man could get with. To this day, we often make salvation a mountain. Tell us how much higher we need to climb, how we can measure it in ourselves and judge others, and we will zealously jump to it.

From this champ's perspective, Jesus presented him with an unfamiliar, more difficult path. Jesus recommended that the rich dude strip himself of his riches and, subsequently, relinquish the space in his mind that identified with and fought to maintain those riches. The young man just couldn't.

Of course, we'd like to think that we'd be different. That had we been given the choice between following this new, audacious religious leader and maintaining our pace up the mountain, we would have chosen Jesus. Thank God for grace though because if I'm honest, I doubt I would have done any different from the young man.

The invitation to be closer to God goes out to everyone, including the young rich guy and all the climbers who can relate, but sometimes it is the money itself, the climb itself, that keeps us from truly following Christ and enjoying the benefits of a life with Him.

A few verses after the young man walked away, Jesus foreshadowed the ultimate salvation plan when He told His disciples that "with man [earning salvation] is impossible, but with God all things are possible" (Matthew 19:26). Today, we can accept salvation in a way this young man couldn't. Because of grace, all we've got to do is confess and believe in Christ. Our faith changes our status, and His Spirit does the work within us (Romans 10:9–10). Because of Christ's finished work on the cross, we can spend too much bandwidth, time, and energy on the mountain and *still* manage to get to heaven. But one thing does remain consistent between the young man and us: We can still miss Him, miss His leading, and miss His promises when we remain too attached to the climb.

Turns out, while the invitation to salvation is for everyone, the promises of God that come *after* salvation— the peace that surpasses understanding, eternal hope, intimacy with God, strength, and rest—are meant for the sons and daughters of God. Did you get that?

Jesus explained to a well-intentioned Nicodemus in John 3:3 that "no one can see the kingdom of God unless they are born again." This rebirth is a spiritual one that is unencumbered by our physical birth. Bosses, stars, workers—all climbers—can accept the invitation to be saved, but then they are born again as children of God.

And it is from *that* identity we receive and experience God's promises. The Bible and human experience show us that while our names may be written in the Lamb's Book of Life, bound for heaven, we can absolutely live in a world marked by stress, anxiety, depression, isolation, lack, and loneliness *still*. I suggest that, for many of us, it is because we live in a world centered around the mountain *still*.

Sons and daughters still go and do incredible things on this earth. They win elections. They buy homes, start families, and build businesses. The amazing thing about being the salt of the earth is that we can be scattered all over the place, in the common market and in the high, elite places. We are bound to succeed at something, accomplish something, and achieve as a part of God's plan. And we are not going to see this manifest until we get on our mountains, study, research, envision, execute, perfect, and protect our assignments.

That said, we can never forget that our identity, our rest, and our ability to live abundantly doesn't lie in *doing* anything. It lies in that humble, simple valley mindset where titles, accolades, and achievement are secondary and who we are as God's son or daughter is primary.

"Pastor" is great, but "son of God" is better. "Boss" is beautiful, but "his daughter" is better. "Stars" will fade, but membership in God's family endures. No multi-hyphenate will ever add up to "child of God." Somewhere in those hyphens, though, the understanding, the trust, and the humility of that divine identity often get lost.

> Perhaps it's time to discover and get better acquainted with learning the true measure of life, satisfaction, and alignment by starting the climb down.

We have lots of experience working up to something. Perhaps it's time to discover and get better acquainted with learning the true measure of life, satisfaction, and alignment by starting the climb down.

CHAPTER 5

MAKE A SACRIFICE OF PAUSE

That new middle school with the Bid Whist and serious dating in fifth grade wasn't like most other public schools. The quintessential Chicago public school, like the one across the street from my house, was marred by Midwest lawlessness, segregation, and academic mediocrity. But this new school required an entrance exam and attracted some of the brightest kids from around the city. I don't know if they still give schools titles like this anymore—it seems pretty classical and stuffy—but this school was known as the Keller *Gifted* Center.

It was my destiny. My family says I could read at two years old, and by four I was grilling mom on trivia. Throughout elementary school I was regularly finishing tests early, waging intellectual battles with the teachers, winning spelling bees, and driving everyone crazy. I even played the drums and the piano, so this new school for the "gifted" had my name written all over it.

I was always expected to be smart. I was always told I was precocious. I was always labeled as "gifted."

I didn't know myself apart from this special status, this special brain, and the special things I could produce with it. That isn't problematic as a kid. Looking back, it certainly felt like a pedestal, but one I was trained to think was normal. It was normal to win, normal to succeed, normal to impress, and normal to score high. It became an integral part of my identity and a persona I thought I had to live up to.

If we think back over our childhoods, most of us would see we were primed to climb the mountain the way we eventually did. I may not have had a true purpose or career or assignment yet, but even nine-year-old Jonathan had a hard time separating his intrinsic, God-given value from his feats of so-called greatness. To be myself was to be great. But it wasn't founded in something bigger than me. It felt like the greatness was completely up to and generated by me.

So by the time I arrived at my mountain later in life, "up" was all I'd known. "Better" was where I was comfortable landing. "More" was all I was comfortable accomplishing. This desire and expectation to be great had little root in being a son of *God*. It was a *personal* charge, and the defining quality of my identity. When it came to academics and music and athletics, I rarely, if ever, lived from the valley up.

The climb that I've come to know and love—and hate— may have begun in 2010, but this climber was missing out on a valley mindset, at least a decade earlier.

This was going to be a long journey for me—and uncomfortable too.

I wish the road to the valley was as nourishing and encouraging as the valley itself. But ironically—obviously— the road to the valley is *still the mountain*.

Assess the Damage

After the stoup meltdown (remember that?), the first step I took toward this valley mindset was to simply stop climbing.

That is such a basic-sounding concept. But it wasn't as simple as clocking out. Or putting the baby to bed or bringing her to Grandma's. Or taking a vacation, a warm bath, or a much-needed nap.

I needed to truly, for one moment, prioritize my heart over the mountain. My soul over my status.

I know what some of you must be thinking. *Who can afford to just cease climbing?* Trust me, I get it. I *still* had to handle responsibilities. I still had to make money and work. It's just that I stopped *needing* to ascend to the next level, or even maintain the progress I had already earned. As soon as I stopped trying to expand, enlarge, win, prove myself, or sustain my career and what I thought was my God-given assignment, I was able to evaluate myself truthfully.

An old gospel song says, "I looked at my hands and they looked new."[1] The lyricist was referring to the new life we can receive in Christ. But when I looked at my hands, after years of climbing, they looked frail and scarred. And my feet were bleeding through my socks.

Immediately, for a couple of months, I chased church services, healing retreats, and mentors. I don't recommend you follow suit entirely, as I tend to do too much sometimes. Some of the trips were not very fruitful. Frankly, the extra travel beat me down even further. I still, however, saw myself coming into *progressive awareness* of the condition the mountain had left me in. Physically. Mentally. Emotionally. Spiritually.

For one, I was tired. The kind of tired that didn't feel like rappelling to relief. The kind of tired that sits in the driveway after a long day because there isn't enough strength available to walk into the house just yet. Professional mountaineers are unified in their observation that accidents happen on the way down; for one, this happens because climbers use most of their energy to ascend the mountain, not realizing that half the battle is climbing back down to earth—and living to tell the tale.

Possibly since childhood, likely for my entire career, but surely for at least those last six years, my only goal was *up*. And maybe even more precisely, my goal was *anything but down*.

And through it all my body was finding new ways to show how stressful it was.

The digestive issues? Gastroenterologist said, "It's stress."

The headaches? Neurologist determined, "stress."

The depression? Therapist cited "stress."

The nerve pain? Eastern medicine doctor pointed to "stress."

The extreme fatigue? Yup, stress. Google took care of that diagnosis.

The only doctor who pointed to anything else was my chiropractor. He believes everything is caused by a misaligned spine. Then again, even the muscles that struggled to hold my skeleton up were being weakened by the frequently required, stressful postures of my work, travel, and performances.

Now that I think about it, everyone's mountain requires a routine of certain *postures*. For me that included a seated posture on countless four-hour flights. It's just sitting, but after a while, the muscles and bones involved become worn-out and overused—and other muscles are neglected. For a lot of us, our most frequent "mountain posture" is hunching over a computer screen. For others, it's being up on your feet and somehow walking miles every day without realizing it. A mother's biceps must grow ridiculously strong after holding her infant—and then toddler—for days and weeks straight. Police officers learn to run toward the gunshots and the drama that everyone else is running *from*. I can imagine that requires a certain compartmentalization the average human doesn't possess. I know that during my tour meet and greets, my face would hurt from the huge smile I had to maintain for an hour of pictures and expectations. All these frequent, though necessary, postures impact us. What postures are required for your climb?

Regardless of the mountain you climb, there is a posture your body, your mind, and your heart must assume to ascend successfully and withstand the higher altitudes. And if you're anything like me, after a while, that body, mind, and heart will take turns demonstrating how those postures have affected you. There's an overworking of some muscle groups and a neglect of the others. Your hip flexors stiffen because of your sedentary life sitting at your desk. You accumulate unresolved trauma from all you absorbed just to do your job. I was wounded from the constant posture of transparency and service to people who were ill-equipped to give me any love back.

That was the physical. That was the mental. But soon the deepest elements of the matter would be unearthed. There was emotional damage. And, yes, there was major spiritual damage too.

I had grown a bit bitter on the mountain. I was mad at God because I felt so much distance from Him. I was mad at people because I didn't feel *enough* distance from them. And all this when I was living, sacrificing, and climbing, I thought, for God and people.

They are the best and the worst you've created
Loving and hating and opinionated
Loners in basements and those congregated
Deliver me from . . . people.[2]

I didn't know it was possible until a decade ago, but I cared way too much about people!

I cared too much about their opinions and where they landed and what taste was left in their mouths. And it wasn't just some people-pleasing mechanism in my heart that needed their love and affirmation. No, it was because as an artist, as a "religious influencer," and (especially) as a *product*, people's thoughts truly do determine my commercial and social success.

I can hear the Church gasping now.

Yes, God is in control of everything; I know that. Still, he doesn't use Spotify and therefore is not directly responsible for streaming numbers and charting on Billboard. Ultimately, for believers and nonbelievers, to track, manage, and predict people's responses and feelings is a crucial part of any marketer's life.

At various parts of the climb, especially early on, people will follow you, they will praise you, and the impact you make on them will be visible. Your success can feel like God's approval, and God's approval seems to be voiced through the crowd's approval. It doesn't take long to mix up the voices, constantly looking for God's smile in the smiles of the public. Or feeling God's neglect when the crowd forsakes you. Leaders, artists, fans, pastors, and entrepreneurs have their own unique battle interpreting God with or against the crowd's opinion. It's an extra weight we carry up the mountain causing the extra damage during the climb.

In Matthew 16:24, Jesus told His disciples that if they wanted to follow Him, they would have to "take up their cross," which meant being down for anything—even death— for the cause of Christ. While every believer has their cross to bear, being a gospel artist, it felt like mine had to be a pristine, universally agreed-upon "cross." My cross wasn't just self-denial for Christ's sake. I didn't suffer too much being persecuted by the *world* for my beliefs. My cross to bear was characterized by self-denial, self-editing, and long-suffering for *Christians'* sake. My life felt like it was more about dodging or enduring persecution from the *Church*. It went past receiving salvation, conquering temptation, and studying the Word. It was also *looking* the part and surviving being judged through several thousand different interpretations of modesty, purity, leadership, and ministry. I don't regret my efforts to live a life above reproach, despite how impossible that seems to be in today's cancel culture. Being aware of a culture's ticks helps you navigate it, find favor in it, and make impact within it.

But it *was* something extra to carry.

And my back screamed.

Minorities, particularly Black people in America, often joke about how we have felt required to change the tone of our voice, our word choices, our natural hairdos, and our fashion ideas to be seen as properly educated, qualified, and ready for a job. Similarly, in the public forum where Baptist, Evangelical, Pentecostal, and everything else meets, I had to adjust a few things to be seen as saved, qualified, and reverent. For example, I pierced my ears freshman year of college, but for fear of being criticized and thought less of, I let the holes close until recently. It had nothing to do with the state of my heart, my allegiance to God, or my seriousness about the call. Reasonable paranoia or not, it became another load that got heavier as I ascended the mountain.

In this age of "church hurt" where we are collectively revealing or becoming aware of the abuses, the secrets, and the outright lovelessness found in some of our local churches, I still don't know if anyone has been hurt as much as the leaders, influencers, and workers whose lives are truly, and for a long time, framed, boxed in, and cramped by service to the church. I shrunk my life and accelerated my climb to rise above people's opinions, expectations of my fall, hesitant acceptance of my music, and skeptical projections. I heard—and read—thousands of nuggets of feedback as my once-innocent, green offering was chiseled by their feedback, warranted or unsolicited.

People. They were heavy.

But then *God*.

I felt more used than loved by Him.

I felt like He had pushed me up this mountain of scarcity to plant His flag somewhere high for *others* to see. For *others* to know He existed and loved them. But He neglected to furnish the mountain for *my* livelihood. He wrapped my life around my talent—the musical, marketable part but not my core, an overthinking, restless, nearly fatherless brainiac. I was His tool, His errand boy, His masterpiece, His billboard, His example, His messenger. Everything—that is, everything but His son.

My hands were tattered, my feet looked anything but "new," but my heart was wounded too. God had certainly given me this mountain, but it wasn't always kind to me. And it felt like the climb neglected half of who He had created me to be. I had worked a few muscles to death. And the other muscles had atrophied from lack of use.

I was mad at God because all this hard, unfulfilling work was for Him.

At least, that's the story I told myself.

But when I stopped and peeled back the ministry title, the Christian messaging, and the noble, positive undertones, I realized much of this climb was for *me*, driven by my own insecurities, doubts, and hopes for my legacy. God may have initiated the climb to complete a few quests, but I was staying on the mountain for *me*. I was trying to escape mediocrity and stay above the people's reproach. I was trying to earn a father and earn intimacy. I was trying to legitimize my feelings of specialness with special feats.

So, maybe *I* was using *Him*.

Make a Sacrifice

I was only a few months removed from screaming about the size of the potatoes in my beef stew, canceling my entire December slate, and receiving my Valley Starter Kit when I started searching for help getting down the mountain.

I crawled across town to the house of a big brother in the faith. I was exhausted. A little angry. Definitely empty.

He, a brilliant, hardworking, multi-hyphenate pastor in LA, had already been down this road of exhaustion and discouragement—plenty of times. Even further, he had watched countless colleagues go down this road too—and crash.

"I think you're about to burn out, bro," he warned, letting a bit of his Mississippi drawl slip through his otherwise polished Hollywood diction. "It's one thing to be tired and a little depressed, but I sense you're really close to hitting the wall."

Christian Talk 101. When pastors are careful to say they "sense" something, as opposed to just *predict, think,* or *feel* something, they are trying to convey that God is potentially giving them insight that we should take a little more seriously. So I let the gravity of his words push me deeper into his cold, leather couch.

The pastor continued to tell me how he had watched several friends "tap their adrenals"—that is, force their body into sustained and pressurized high performance—over and over again to deliver powerful sermons, manage multiple services, travel, play politics, and counsel couples. He offered that we tend to think that adrenaline, that energy, is of unlimited supply, but it truly is, like everything about us, finite. And without proper rest—more than just a good night's sleep—that supply can run out. He described great men and women who could barely get out of bed for a year as the roof collapsed on the life, altitude, and rhythm they'd once known.

His words resonated with me. As he spoke, I even got a mild pain in my side, where I imagined my adrenal gland was, aching out of concern. Through this almost-divine message from my friend and mentor, I could also imagine that I was on the verge of hitting an unprecedented, serious wall.

So, right in that moment, I started to mentally assign a couple of weeks in the late summer to get off the mountain and meet God. The fourteen days were nestled conveniently between the end of touring season and the beginning of, well, another touring season. If God could really show me something incredible in the time allotted, I could have another productive annual climb! Typical mountain-man mindset.

"I think mid-July to the beginning of August would work," I confidently proposed.

He shook his head and chuckled. I could sense he was *sensing* stuff again. Of course, he argued, "No. I think God is going to need more of a sacrifice out of you."

He was right.

I was structuring my valley time based on my mountain mindset. My first instinct was that this rediscovery of Jonathan as son would first have to bow to who I was as an artist, boss, and uncle. God, and time with Him, needed to jibe with my schedule, as well as the climb I still allowed to define me.

I could have—and *you* can right now—prayed and done my best to be still and psych myself into five minutes of not thinking about work, but truly walking back down to the valley, stripping myself of this chronic mountain mindset, and living *from* the valley was going to take a while. It was going to take a *sacrificial* approach to sabbatical. A sacrificial use of my off time. A sacrificial reprioritization of values.

It's not uncommon to hear believers bring a monetary sacrifice to God. We look at our account balance, sigh, and ponder our next faith move. It's not uncommon to hear a worship leader encourage us to bring a sacrifice of praise. So we force out one more "Hallelujah" early Sunday morning when what we're really looking forward to is the post-service nap. It's a lot less common to hear about a sacrifice of *pause*. That would require us to ask ourselves if stopping to look inward and hear God is tenable, even if it may cost us progress up the mountain.

I had a big tour coming up in April, and I needed to figure out something—and fast. All I could think of were the stories of nervous breakdowns, videos of wild rants on the mic, and the blurry, overexposed paparazzi photos of celebrities who had gone insane on the mountain. What would a breakdown look like for me? Would I cuss out a random fan in the VIP line for giving me weird energy? Would I cancel certain nights of my tour so I could escape to urgent care? Would I get a little too honest onstage and say something strange that would go viral?

I didn't want to find out. So, while the plan was to sacrifice the end of the year, after the tour, and give God a lot more time and energy and pause, I needed to do something now. Quickly. Before I made a complete spectacle of myself.

Here I was, as winter turned to spring, trying to get ahold of myself, pausing the climb, and coming into progressive awareness of how much I had been hurting. However, the scars and the injuries I was becoming aware of weren't just from my own weight. I'd been under two hundred pounds for most of this journey, but my bones ached as if I'd weighed hundreds more.

Did you know, on newer iPhones you can use driving mode and send a custom automatic message to anyone who texts you? Well, after a carefully worded mass message that I sent to the people who were the most important to me—and the people who drained me the most—I set my phone to simply reply "Mental health break. Pray."

I began to descend. Clumsily. Uncertainly. With questions. But I was coming down.

Be Intentional, Even in Uncertainty

As God showed me these concepts of mountain mindsets and valley thinking, I became a fly on the wall of forums among professional climbers. I'd watch videos on YouTube and read Quora chats. From rock climbers to amateur mountaineers, I watched them as they argued over many things—best practices, the difficulty of certain mountains, and whether they believed some of the local legends they'd encountered. They were at odds about many things, but they all could agree that climbing down, in many ways, was scarier and more uncomfortable than climbing up.

There's a "greater feeling of exposure."[3]

It's "harder to see footholds."[4]

We've "practiced it less."[5]

Whatever invincibility, power, and safety we feel while facing the mountain on the way up is washed away when we're looking down, doing something less natural and less rehearsed.

Rather than might, it takes a lot of faith, patience, and focus.

Rather than a constant fight against gravity, we're giving gravity more sway.

I had to be intentional the entire way. Even though I was completely uncertain as to what would happen if I made myself "of no reputation" (Philippians 2:7 NKJV) and came down from my knockoff brand of glory. More than anything, it would take faith—that God is real. That He thinks of me as His child, wants me home, and will draw near to me as I draw near to Him.

> Whatever invincibility, power, and safety we feel while facing the mountain on the way up is washed away when we're looking down, doing something less natural and less rehearsed.

The next season of life would be about walking downhill, looking for safe ways down, rappelling from cliffs, and, while dangling my feet below me, searching for the next foothold.

CHAPTER 6

LEARN THE WAY BACK DOWN

The process of walking downhill may be foreign and frightening to most of you because all you've known is the climb. The way up is more natural to you. I get it. The climb feels purposeful, and it keeps us from idle thought. We have accepted loneliness, exhaustion, mood swings, shallow relationships, and paranoia as normal. The thought of a different kind of life and contentment and support sounds good but impossible. We may not do it enough, but a *temporary* pause in the climb, a deceleration of the grind and the hustle, is, at least, familiar. A day at the spa. Or a weeklong vacation. Or leaving the kids with Grandma for the day. Normally, we can wrap our heads around that and then go massage, beach, or TV our way to a little pause.

Climbing down, however, requires a bit more work but is essential for the balance of life and health. It is a treasure given to anyone who believes in the Giver. A treasure to anyone who believes a relationship with Him is priceless. A treasure that rivals any treasure we'd earn on the mountain.

This treasure of sonship and daughterhood, of resting in God's finished work, can only be found in the valley. When you come down and live from that mindset, everything you ever do on the mountain afterward will be empowered by a different divine strength and certainty.

Life from the valley.

I wanted this valley for myself. Staggering down an unbeaten path took longer than I'd hoped and revealed things in me I wasn't proud of, but every step was worth it. On the mountain, we use our eyes and our feet to find or feel for a safe step down. I'm going to tell you about the footholds I found that you can reach down for daily, weekly, or seasonally to get back down from your high place. Prayerfully, we can get into a better rhythm, where daily and weekly we descend back into our Father's arms.

Gracefully accepting the descent keeps us gratefully appreciating our ascent.

Step #1: Shut That Ego Up!

When I sat down to map my journey, I realized that every step down had a pattern. No doubt it's a cautious walk down the slopes—left foot, pause, right foot, pause—while desperately inhaling and exhaling the thickening air. A particular rhythm is required to descend successfully.

Less reliance on and appeasing of me.

More remembrance of God.

Less of me.

More of God.

Less of me.

More of God.

The first step for us all is, undoubtedly, less *ego*. Whether we want to admit it or not, ego—our sense of self-esteem, identity, and self-importance—is typically half the reason we are up so high in the first place. Rarely do purpose, assignment, or service push you up there by themselves.

When I was around ten or eleven years old, growing up in the church, I regularly challenged myself to be like the adults. They had special fasts sometimes, and I figured I was old enough to participate too. I don't think my prepubescent body was ready to deal with the hunger pangs and sudden lack of sugar, but I was up for the challenge. Or so I thought. Whenever the church mothers—think ornate dresses and big hats, elderly and sweet but passing out tough rebukes—noticed how moody and cranky I was midfast, they'd admonish me to give up and grab the Snickers, because "God would rather you eat than act ungodly." If your mountain mindset has you losing the fruit of the Spirit, there's a chance He didn't demand such heights. I bet you I know what did, though! *Ego.* And to get "down" to sonship or daughterhood, you're going to need to address it.

Each step down this mountain should register as *less of me, more of God, less of me, more of God.* Our culture unintentionally—or intentionally—moves God out of the center of our journeys and, at best, only retains Him as a means to another end. We often don't pray to end up with God, but rather to end up rich, successful, or happy . . . with God's help. The mountain mindset that is self-centered, wealth-oriented, and preoccupied with pleasure and pleasant feelings is not tethered to anything any more powerful than the person climbing it. Disappointment or emptiness is inevitable. We've seen it a million times!

So how does one shrink the powerful force of ego? Quiet the inner voices that our egos amplify? There are a few that shout the loudest. Like the one voice that warns us of the misleading formula that lost time equals lost progress.

Back in my cranky fasting days, every morning before I ran out to the school bus stop, my mom would stop me at the door to pray. And every time I'd roll my eyes but oblige. But one day, I woke up late and in a panic. I rushed to gather the homework from the previous night and stuff it into my backpack. I glanced at the clock, ran through the living room, and threw my coat on midstride. Mom was waiting at the door, but instead of opening it and launching me out into the cold Chicago morning, she stopped to pray with me.

"Mom, I'm gonna miss the bus!"

"If praying makes you late, you were going to be too early."

I need you to get that: If praying makes you late, you were going to be too early.

If going home to the valley and engaging with God as His son or daughter causes you to be late or lose progress, be thankful, for perhaps you would have been somewhere at the wrong time.

Successfully climbing tall mountains like Everest is not a straight shot up. Mountaineers use the adage "Climb high, sleep low."[1] The goal is to gain altitude during the day but sleep at lower altitudes to acclimate to the thin air. Climbers make multiple trips up and down before summiting, including at least three trips up from and down to base camp.[2] To ascend from a low altitude to the highest altitude without establishing a patient

> If going home to the valley and engaging with God as His son or daughter causes you to be late or lose progress, be thankful, for perhaps you would have been somewhere at the wrong time.

rhythm of coming back down before your next run higher pretty much guarantees brain and lung swelling and, you guessed it, death. Steve Pearson, who climbed Everest with our boy Roskelley, put it like this: "Sometimes we expect life to have a constant direction, but that's not how it works. There are ups and downs, and the downs are an essential part of eventually reaching the top. You can't be discouraged by the fact that you had to come down a little. That is part of the process to be able to go higher."[3]

Pure professional mountain climbing still requires coming down. Any upward progress without trips down to reacclimate is in vain. This rings even more urgently for the human *life* that was never meant to completely center around climbing the mountain anyway. This is regardless of what your ego wants you to do.

Busting the ego requires quieting the ego's chant of the myth of lost time and lost progress. If God is sovereign and

potent enough, and the sum of our lives is rooted in closeness and obedience to Him, time off the mountain to be
with Him will *not* count against you. Now, time away from
climbing to do *other* things may, but time climbing down,
stripping yourself of titles, and basking in your divine sonship or daughterhood will not.

In the book of Joel, God exhibited His mastery over
what was thought to be lost or wasted time and progress. "I
will repay you for the years the locusts have eaten—the great
locust and the young locust, the other locusts and the locust
swarm—my great army" (Joel 2:25). If God had the ability
to make up for the years of famine and natural destruction
Israel suffered through, certainly he can restore the months,
the weeks, the days, or the minutes that we stop our climb
to go back down.

Unfortunately, even when the myth of lost progress
is outed, sometimes the ego won't let up. And with social
media, it gets a 4.8-billion-speaker sound system to scream
through.[4] Facebook—and all the social media apps—has
created several major problems for society to figure out or
live with. It is a soapbox for anyone and everyone. The most
ridiculous opinions, takes, and information can significantly
affect culture, politics, and everything in between. It's most
problematic because of its inflating and deflating effects on
the aforementioned ego. It cultivates constant discouragement, constant performance evaluation, constant pressure to
stay on the mountain to have, if nothing else, something to
post. And most of all, it causes constant comparison.

After quieting the lying narrative of lost time and progress, the second chant of ego that you may need to turn down is one of comparison.

That fateful December evening after combusting over dinner, I canceled starring in a movie I had previously agreed to. That was heartbreaking enough, but a decision is a decision. As I started down my mountain, though, I had to deal with the reality of my role being filled by someone else. Not only did I feel like I was missing out and threatening my professional track record, I had to watch someone else climb past me. There was a moment when I considered getting back to the grind and making up, not for lost progress or time, but for lost pole position—lost advantage and lost place in the imaginary race I was running against . . . I guess, *everyone*.

When I was about five, despite it technically being illegal, I was occasionally allowed to sit in the front passenger seat. And I remember pressing an imaginary gas pedal as my aunt drove down the highway. I would watch the other cars driving and try to *will* our car ahead of everyone. My aunt didn't know she was in a race. And the other cars certainly didn't know when they were winning or losing. The race was entirely in my head. The other cars on the road weren't even going the same place. Some were exiting in a mile. Others were on a very long interstate trip. Some were big trucks full of people and equipment. Other vehicles were meant for speed and show. But there I was, putting myself and my aunt's Pontiac Grand Prix in a drag race no one was participating in but me. Almost three decades later, I was doing the same thing. Though God was behind the wheel, I was pushing an imaginary pedal, hoping He wouldn't let me get beat.

As you wind down your mountain mindset, you may see others ascending. Fight the urge to catch back up. Faith in God's timing, individual timing, His grace, individual grace, must conquer the pangs of your ego that tell you your life is measured in how it compares to someone else's.

It's a lie.

And you must treat it as such.

Allow me to offer another helpful perspective, and with it, three ego-shushing statements.

Consider that well-known story in the Bible about the tempting of Jesus. After forty days of fasting, Jesus was led by the Spirit into the desert to be tempted by the devil. The devil tried to entice Him in three different ways.

First, he tried to get Jesus to give up the divinely ordained fast and miraculously turn stones into lunch for Himself. I'm sure food would have been quite nice, and Jesus was definitely *capable* of this feat, but Jesus understood that what He was after was greater and responded to the devil saying, "It is written: 'Man shall not live on bread alone, but on every word that comes from the mouth of God'" (Matthew 4:4).

Second, the devil took Him to a high point in the city and asked Jesus to throw Himself down to the ground in expectation that, because of His *importance* and *invincibility*, angels would come and save Him. Jesus responded, "It is also written: 'Do not put the Lord your God to the test'" (Matthew 4:7).

Lastly, the devil showed Jesus all the kingdoms of the world, their splendor and wealth. The devil told Jesus that if He'd bow down and worship the devil, all that wealth and success would be His. Jesus quickly shouted back, "For it is written: 'Worship the Lord your God, and serve him only'" (Matthew 4:10).

Now imagine if "the devil" weren't an outside entity. Imagine if he weren't a separate character, with horns or a red body or a striking countenance, but simply a manifestation of Jesus' *ego*. Imagine if that entire war was in Jesus' head. Suddenly, the way He was tempted becomes a lot more familiar and relatable to us. We may not have had a masquerading "angel of light" show up and look us in the face, but we *have* had our ego masquerade as an enlightening, protecting angel of light inside our own heads.

When this *devil*—the one outside or the one inside— shows up and plays to our sense of capability and skill, we must respond as Jesus did. The devil hoped to entice Jesus to simply *do* something—do *more*—in His own strength that could change His predicament and address His overwhelming hunger. Jesus responded with a truth grounded in His sense of what was truly needed in life. And nothing was more important to Him than seeking, understanding, and living out the precious Word of God. Similarly, our ego often tells us if we work harder, work some magic, and do more, we can alleviate the hunger we feel. We squash that ego with renewed awareness that what we need is not on the mountain—in the *stones*—but by living from the Word that God has for us in the valley.

So, here's your first ego-shushing line: "Stones? On the mountain?! I can't eat those! I can't live off that!" We can't live off progress up the mountain. We live from the words, the affirmation, the direction that stems from God in the valley. That's the only way any progress on the mountain makes sense. And lost progress is certainly better than lost relationship.

Similarly, when the devil played on Jesus' sense of self-importance and invincibility—the ego—Jesus had to remind him who was truly important and sovereign. I don't care how important you feel you are to the mission, the Kingdom, your job, your family—don't let ego keep you on the mountain playing games with your life. You are not invincible. You are not self-sufficient. And daring God to rescue you while you prove something is not the same as trusting Him enough that you have nothing to prove. Jesus responded, "Don't put the Lord your God to the test." Your ego-shushing line here is, "I'm important, but not *that* important."

The devil saved his best for last, though. Nothing entices people to climb the mountain up to absurd heights more than the idea of potential riches and success. Our ego will absolutely tell us that if we just fixate on the mountain a little more, success is bound to come. Again, there is *nothing* wrong with wanting and pursuing success on Earth. The problem comes with who or what you will bow to in order to get there. Here, the success wasn't worth the cost of success, so Jesus responded vehemently that He'd only be bowing to something true and lasting, the one true God.

Watch what the mountain—and your ego—asks you to bow to. How many yeses does it require? How much reprioritization does it demand? How often do you find yourself bowing to people, compromising values, and submitting to others' thoughts just to be and stay successful on the mountain? Your last ego-busting line? "I want only God's idea of success for me."

God's idea of success for you may include a healthy family, a strong ministry, a competitive company, or a wall full of credentials, but it absolutely will not come at the cost of bowing to anything else. Especially bowing to the ego's devilish voices.

As you finish your workday, your workweek, your Sunday service schedule, or your seasonal projects and aim back down to God's valley of sonship and daughterhood, rehearse those three ego busters:

"Stones? On the mountain?! I can't eat those! I can't live off that!"

"I'm important, but not *that* important."

"I want only God's idea of success for me."

And then see how he's feeling about all your great feats.

To properly come down is to combat the lies your ego will tell you. We combat them with the truth of the gospel and how our agenda fits inside of God's agenda. Not how His fits within ours. Our agenda will always be to get ahead and stay ahead, but His won't always align with that. And we'll have to learn to be OK with not getting as far as fast, or staying ahead, as we'd planned. It's a recurring step-down. The mountain will be OK without you. And you will be OK without the mountain.

Step #2: Remember Your History with God

I don't need an organ to praise Him! I don't need a drum! All I need is a memory.
—A Pentecostal preacher any given Sunday

The second step of coming down the mountain is passing the moments—which are often successful or inspiring moments—that you lived, conquered, and saw God moving on your behalf. A journey of any kind is an amazing miracle. Big feats of progress are all achieved by taking an abundance of small, ordinary steps. It helps to look back and see how far you've come. How much you've gained. How much you've lost. It's good to be reminded of the tough moments that didn't end your climb, destroy your life, or destroy you. Those unpleasant moments may be even *more* revealing, as many of them convinced you to push harder and higher up into the clouds in the first place.

While social media can be a gateway to social comparison, one of its elements aided my descent. Facebook literally keeps everything. All the pictures that I took, that someone else took, that I uploaded, that someone else uploaded are all there—thousands of them. Without buying a photo album, without filling an external drive, Facebook has chronicled my life, my career, and my climb since high school. One day, I was looking for this old picture of me and then-Senator Barack Obama in his old smoke-filled office from, like, I don't know, 2006? As I scrolled back, I saw all these flyers of old concerts and gigs. I saw my hair when it was shorter. My body when it was leaner. Most significantly, I saw my career—my climb—rewound.

There were pictures of events I remember fearing. Immediately, I recalled those crazy, awkward days where I'd have to bring a quiet acoustic guitar to a loud, chaotic choir concert. The sound guys—if they even had sound guys—stared at me, puzzled by how to hook up this odd piece of wood they'd never seen up close before. I remember feeling so out of place, so underneath the moment.

One picture showed me in a rather extravagantly decorated church vestibule. I remember this triumph. The Black, charismatic, Pentecostal church often has a double portion of theatrics and drama. Sometimes it looks, feels, and sounds like a circus. I remember feeling quite small, stiff, and out of place in the pandemonium. Imagine Kenny G with Metallica. Or Josh Groban with Cardi B.

I remember watching as the third rambunctious choir finished their set. They were jamming. Twenty-plus singers, a four-piece band, blowing all the Black church dog whistles and hitting all the right notes. (For instance, the phrase "When I think of the goodness of Jesus and all he's done for me . . ." for some reason connects enthusiastically with Pentecostal congregants and will always result in some extra volume.) The audience of about one hundred people danced and stomped and shouted for fifteen minutes straight. The pews were in shambles. (Understand that I don't mean the pews were broken, but the people in them, moved by the choir's performance, were disheveled, sweating, and pleasantly exhausted.) I thought, *I wish I'd gone before them, but I am so glad I'm not right after them*. I felt sorry for the next performer who had to follow that and sing to the broken pieces of the audience that were left. It was getting late, and it felt like the last bit of energy and attentiveness had been zapped out of the room.

As the choir filed off the stage, I started to wonder how anyone was going to rein in the highly spirited room. I sat glued to my pew, listening to the host either misread or, on impulse, change the order of things and proceed to call me up. I'm not even sure if he said my name right. I walked up sheepishly with my obnoxious, inanimate sidekick—a Taylor acoustic guitar—and looked down at the available cords and outlets on the floor. Before I could even consider myself, I had to consider the room and consider my guitar. I connected my cable in the awkward silence and rushed nervously to the mic.

The rest, I don't remember. But according to this picture I found, I was smiling in the lobby as people asked to take pictures with me. So I guess things went well.

I felt out of place, under the moment. And yet, with God's help, I made it.

This picture was proof of one of many spots in my climb that God allowed me to push through. For me, this moment symbolized an era where I knew even less than I know now. I knew less about the industry. I had less confidence in my delivery and stage presence. I knew less church jargon and social navigation. I *only* made it past that moment by the grace of God. I only made it because He must have been shining a light so bright behind me that it softened the shadows and made my flaws endearing.

For the rest of the night, after I proved that I had met Barack Obama, I walked down memory lane and marveled at God's résumé with me.

With those nostalgic moments, I felt myself coming down farther from my high place on the mountain. My position in life hadn't changed. I hadn't lost any success or reputation. But my mentality was beginning to shift out of pursuit and into gratitude.

Remember, the lower you get, the more evidence of life there is—the life you can have beyond the cares of career and assignment.

We're going to get there one step at a time. Right foot, quiet the ego. Left foot, remember your and God's history.

Step #3: Call Your Nephew

Now it's time to widen our lens, our focus, from the me-centric mountain to the larger, more realistic image of the world around us. As we get farther up our mountains, we get more and more tunnel-visioned, more and more self-absorbed, and a lot less cognizant of how we fit into a larger world, community, and agenda. This third step to coming off the mountain is to consider others and serve your way off the mountain.

I could write another book on the plight and internal fight of artists and entertainers. While we are highly praised and sometimes even highly paid, there is a bipolarity to our lives that often syncs up with a bipolarity and hypersensitivity within us. And good or bad, the earth is becoming full of us "artists," even if some of us are hidden in less traditionally artistic occupations at the moment (bank tellers, pastors, stay-at-home moms, and so on).

The endorphins and extreme sense of alignment when things are going "right" and being well-received are often offset by an extreme sense of doubt, intrusive thoughts, and disarray when things are less postable. Instability has been accepted as an occupational hazard for many artists, living from gig to gig, applause to rejection. Sometimes, that reality pushes artists and entertainers and creators farther up the mountain, as we never know when we could catch—or miss—our big break. We choose never to get caught off the mountain, out of practice, without something new to talk about. The divergence of our minds, the instability of the occupation, and our understandable hyperdrive generally keep us in the clouds much of our lives. Up in the cold, thin air.

I have dealt with a lot of the standard mountain issues I've talked about in this book, and maybe even a few uncommon symptoms too. Like a cloud that formed over me after I read the wrong comment, lost the right opportunity, underachieved a little bit, or was unsure about the future, depression and anxiety hovering six feet above my head. And whenever I was triggered, it wasn't hard for me to feel unloved and unable—and overly dramatic for feeling that way.

While I obviously love and have absorbed the things my mother has told me in more detail than she intended, I still have tried to keep most of these bouts in the cloud away from her. I'm more inclined to tell her what is going on versus how I feel about it.

But one day she must have figured me out. I must have let her in on an anxious moment. I don't normally place these feelings of despair on her doorstep, so I braced myself for her to be extra mother-y and basically baby-talk me back to health and stature.

That's not what happened, though.

She responded to my laundry list of gripes with "Call your nephew."

"What? Why? Is he OK?!"

She answered, "I think so, but you should just call him."

Now, everybody who knows me knows I don't treasure anything more than my nieces and nephew. I love being "Uncle Jonny," so the mention of my nephew, Khalil, stopped me in my tracks. The complaints I had made to my mom, some of those standard mountain issues, were insignificant compared to the idea of Khalil facing even the smallest problem. The cloud hadn't disappeared, but her adding him to my psyche was like a sudden zoom out from my lonely, sad mountain. It's not that my nephew's potential problems became more important than my real ones. It's that I suddenly realized the world didn't revolve around me. I am a main character for my life, but I'm not the only one in the world.

In an instant, I regained a wider perspective. It's as if the blinders I'd been using to focus on the mountain had been ripped off and my peripheral vision showed a much larger picture. It showed a young man who looked up to me. It showed a family, a community, something more than just me and my dogged, selfish pursuit to be amazing.

That main character energy is empowering, for sure, but it also provides a lot of pressure to be the center of every story and every moment. God has intimate, you-focused moments already planned, but in our haste, we constantly manufacture narratives that keep us and our ascent in the spotlight.

Khalil, at the time, was in his late teens or early twenties. Calling my nephew may not—will not—result in some long, beautiful conversation. I normally don't get much more than an "I'm good" out of him. No one is getting therapized or is crying by the end of our verbal exchanges. Calling him wouldn't solve his problems. I may not even give him any advice. I may not grab hold of some profound exchange that changes my day. But calling my nephew, at the very least, widened the image of my life beyond the mountain. It deemphasized my own climb and positioned me back into a community where I belonged, rather than up on my high perch.

High up on the mountain, a lot of us come up with ways, come up with content, come up with messages for the large swath of people *out there*—our fans, our employees, our congregation—who we think need to hear us. There is so much emphasis on that far-reaching value, usefulness, and reception to people who are not in our immediate circles. But that grander external focus comes at the expense of the community, the friends, and the loved ones right under our nose, the people who were assigned to give us a sense of belonging, covering, and identity—and us, them.

Living on the mountain absent of a valley mindset keeps us hyperfocused on our own feet against the rocks and wide-eyed at our own personal kingdom we are building. Too skinny. Too wide. And missing the people stuck between the two. In your immediate sphere. On your block. In your living room. Including your own nephew.

This third step of service, which should divert attention away from the server, is an antidote to the egocentricity the climb encourages. Engage with someone new in your community. Volunteer—gladly—at your local church. Pitch in where there's a gap to clean up or teach. Spend your time and money on something other than sustaining the climb. Move your own self-preservation from the center of your brain. Push it a little to the left so you can let some oxygen in.

This can get tricky if your climb is connected to service. If you're a mother. A pastor. A teacher. Many of us feel our lives are already full of service. Perhaps you are already giving to people, already volunteering at a soup kitchen, already performing funeral services, already caring for kids. The objective of service is not simply to serve *down*. I've observed that no matter what your vocation or part of your calling is, when your service and engagement is primarily pointed down to your dependent children, down to fans or congregants, down to students and employees, you get pushed higher and higher into rarefied air.

I once had a taping at Brigham Young University in Provo, Utah, one of the most picturesque cities in the world. On the flight there, I sat next to a young white guy wearing a fresh, white-collared shirt and black tie. He had his laptop out and was feverishly typing. I couldn't help but notice a few references to "God" and "Jesus" and inquired what his fuss was about. I learned that he was a Mormon. I couldn't resist engaging further with him. I'm aware of the theological differences between my Protestant faith versus his, and I thought, *This could be fun.* He told me he was preparing a sermon, and I was quite impressed that he was obviously the pastor of a church.

"Wow, so you're the pastor of your . . ." I may have ignorantly said "tribe." (I was embarrassed by my unfamiliarity with his faith and culture. I knew things were different in Mormon culture—just not sure *how* different. I really hope I said "community" or "church.")

"Well, yes and no," he replied. "I am preaching this week, but next week I'll be doing something else."

I thought he was telling me a scandal was about to be exposed and he'd be canceled by his next sermon. I leaned in and asked, "What do you mean?"

"At my church, we kind of do a round-robin-type thing. This week I'm bringing the sermon, next week I may be helping in the kitchen, and the next week, I might be teaching the kids."

I was taken aback. I was so used to the Pentecostal model where the pastor does 95 percent of the preaching. Yes, there are special services, special Sundays, special occasions where other people would get a chance to speak, but he made it seem like this was a normal thing. Who he had to be this Sunday, he wasn't last week, and wouldn't have to be the next.

We began to discuss the engagement and humility that setup fostered throughout the community. And I have to say, I was impressed.

Everyone in his community had to stay equally engaged and, more importantly, no one individual had all the power, weight, and responsibility.

I don't know how well it works. I don't even know if this practice is common throughout his faith or specific to his church. But I did begin to imagine a community where the pastor wasn't saddled with all the impact and duty. A place where pastoring wasn't part of the climb. A church that didn't offer you a particular mountain to conquer. A community that the preacher always felt *a part* of rather than *in charge* of.

It's unfortunate so many of us serve in a community we don't feel a part of. We don't get to just feel responsibility to it; we feel responsibility *for* it.

When your life is oriented in a manner where everyone is beneath you and has a systematic dependence on you, how could you ever be humble and comfortable enough to come down? The goal of "calling your nephew" was not so I could offer advice and save the day. It wasn't calling *down* to him as much as it was calling *over*. It was simply to reconnect me with a community, widen my view of my life, and move my own climb away from the center of my thoughts.

So, bosses, engage with your neighbors, with your family around the house, and see how you can exchange resources or manpower.

Pastors, go to another church incognito, sit in the regular seats, and just enjoy it. Better yet, find another department, another role in your church and sit in for a while. Clean up. Watch the kids. Get off your perch.

Artists, leave the studio and immerse yourself in a friend's side hustle. Just help for a night.

Moms, encourage another mom. Remind her she's probably doing a lot better than she feels she is.

Social media influencer . . . well, you should try serving at the soup kitchen. Just try not to post about it.

Step #4: Shut Up and Talk

One foot. Less of me. Check the ego.

Next foot. More of God. Check His résumé.

Right foot. Less of me. Call your nephew.

Left foot. More of God. Get still. Call God.

The fourth step in your descending pattern requires—surprise, surprise—your commitment to the discipline of prayer, including being still. The final movement in this descent is being still and learning—or relearning—how to talk to God. I am not proud of how little I prayed as I worked atop my mountain. I was doing everything else but praying. And the few times I did pray, I was in stride. I treated prayer like a religious discipline I ought to check off the list every day—or every few days. There was no intentionality. No press. No listening. And definitely no stillness.

I always assumed I was a man of God, a man of faith, and, therefore, a man of prayer. By virtue of what I did, the way people saw me and my continued success, I assumed I was being enough of the man of prayer I needed to be. One day, during the summer touring season—well before my burnout and descent—while running around for last-minute equipment, I approached a red light. I crawled up to the white line before the intersection, clenched my eyes tight like a five-year-old saying grace, and dropped my chin into my chest. After peeking through my eyelids a couple of times to make sure the light hadn't changed, I began to pray: "Lord, I thank you . . ." As I continued to move my lips, tongue, and jaw in sync, my brain scrambled to send unfamiliar signals to my face. Suddenly, it hit me—I had not prayed in a long time.

My heart dropped. Here I was, representing God every day, claiming to be one of His sons and doing work in His name, but I hadn't regularly talked to Him. It's amazing how we can do things *for* God but forget to do things *with* Him.

Still stopped at the red light, I shook my head in disappointment. I was disappointed in myself for how far I had obviously fallen, even as I'd been ascending the mountain. Finally, I began again. I hadn't gotten far, listing the things I was grateful for, before I heard the rumble of an engine. My head swooped up, and I instinctively released my foot from the gas pedal.

False alarm. That car was just turning left.

I went back to my cute list, but this time keeping my eyes open in anticipation of the light change. After I drove off, I remember my mind quickly dividing its conscious bandwidth first in half—prayer and driving. Then in thirds—prayer, driving, and navigation. Then prayer, driving, navigation, and my destination. And then this song in my head. And what I needed to add to the to-do list. And the to-do list itself. And the evaluation of my terrible prayer. And the shame of my terrible prayer life. By half a mile, I had quit on the prayer altogether.

I imagine most Christians, especially the ones from the Western world, would agree that God hears our prayers whether we're on our knees at our bedside or running to Kinko's. (I will call that place Kinko's forever. I don't care.) But do *we* hear them? Are we consciously talking to our Father in heaven or just religiously spouting something into the air? If His ears are always keen to our petitions, are we even careful to request the right thing when our mind is so divided? And will we remember what we just requested in case it is granted? And are our ears primed for His answer?

Back then, most of my prayers happened in the car while I rushed dangerously from one errand to another. From the driver's seat, I could ask God a question, but I also regularly asked Him to give me a sign. But not like a quiet biblical word or something subtle. I'm talking *obvious*! I'd start looking around, hoping a billboard or the sky or the sun or the slow tractor trailer *that wouldn't get out of the way* had my answer plastered on it. Perhaps a plane could skywrite "NO" really quick before I turned into this parking lot and signed this contract.

As a matter of fact, my most frequent prayer was, "Lord, if this is not meant for me, don't let it happen." What I was *actually* doing was probably just mentally preparing myself for LA traffic to make me miss my flight. The more I refused to pause my climbing to focus on being in relationship with God, the bigger and more obvious and disruptive I needed the sign to be. And I don't think I need to remind you how dangerous that can be. I've always lived by the idea that God shows (Romans 1:20), whispers (1 Kings 19:11–13), speaks (1 Samuel 3:1–10, Exodus 3, plus all the biblical prophets), but also yells (Acts 9:3–4). And when I was on that climb, unwilling to pause even for a second, the more often He'd have to yell in order for me to hear Him.

Let's assume that God is always present and engaged with our prayers. But as we run around, dividing our minds like a kid's birthday sheet cake, are we present and engaged?

Are we primed for transformation, discipline, and direction? We may be ready for the answer to flash in front of our eyes like an orange LED construction sign, but are we truly able to hear a still, small whisper? Or even to see what He's already been showing us?

The prayers in stride are probably better than nothing, I guess. But they are not likely potent enough to live off of. I can't say that my broken twenty-second prayer reminded me that I was God's son. I can't say that I let Him give me peace. I can't say that I remembered much of what I said, nor what I heard. My prayers were certainly not set up to produce much fruit—spiritual food I desperately needed on this mountain. However, it was a start. And if that's what you can manage right now, by all means, do it. Just don't settle.

It took an interview to make the lightbulb flash for me.

I sat on a hard, orange sofa as a couple interviewed me for their podcast. At that point, I had taken my first few steps down from the mountain, but I couldn't help that my new album was coming out soon and a tour was being promoted. Press was unavoidable. I sat there with a mask on, *acting* rested, *acting* like a climber. I'm normally poised, searching for effortless-sounding profundities. They didn't know I was descending, caring less about my image or their opinions and ready to give the rawest answers. They asked me about my creative process. And I gave them what they wanted, one of my typical funny but accurate answers.

"Most of my songs are written in three places: the car, the shower, or the toilet. Now you decide which songs are which, but one of the songs is called 'Make Room.'" (You're supposed to laugh. Toilet? Make room? OK, never mind.)

Even if you didn't laugh, they laughed, and I went on to say, "Basically, those are the times I'm still."

Ding!

The best things I've created, the times I've heard from God to write a song for His people to sing, were inspired while I was still.

If I had no other reason to trust that the Holy Spirit works with me, my songwriting and career are proof. And when I access Him for music, for lyrics, and for revelation, I must be still. So why not give Him that access for life?

In the shower, in the driver's seat, and on the porcelain throne, I am still. For once, the bulk of my energy, physical and mental, is not being expended to climb, to accomplish, or to build. All of a sudden, I can hear from heaven.

I had to learn to practice that same stillness, that same sacredness, that same space I gave music to simply give . . . God.

Stop. Don't move. Listen to music, but only if it's not distracting. Only if it reminds you of God and His attributes—goodness, mercy, love, peace, joy, etc. And just be.

Thank Him.

Ask of Him.

Honor Him.

Believe that He heard you.

And listen to Him.

And resist the urge to fix, continue, progress, climb, accomplish, or achieve anything. You already have. You reminded your soul that you are His.

And Repeat

I am not marketing these four steps as some one-size-fits-all route to peace and freedom. This isn't a money-back-guarantee rehabilitative program into God's arms. But it is a cycle of movement, a rhythm of discipline and action that can walk you back down into sonship or daughterhood. Continue to exhale self and inhale God, one step at a time, until you make it home to the valley.

CHAPTER 7

TAKE IN THE VIEW

It was eight months after I'd freaked out over *stoup*, canceled shows, and paused the climb. Six months of checking my ego, walking down memory lane, serving my way down, and learning stillness and prayer.

I had embarked on an experiment of sorts. LA, which was a bit of an experiment, too, treated me well, but I never saw myself settling in a grossly overpriced home with no real yard in the hills nor in the valley. I had known the California life for three years, the artist life for twelve, and the bachelor life for . . . ever. But I wanted to see if I could perceive the next step, the next stage of life, career, and love from a different vantage point.

So, I bought a country house on the East Coast.

More yard than house. Quaint. No sense in emptying the bank account for an experiment.

Well water.

One-lane roads.

And quiet, except for the rumble of the RV generators

and the occasional distant pop of shotgun-owning neighbors engaging in a little target practice.

A far cry from the Southside of Chicago or the Hollywood streets I was used to.

I've heard that some people take months or even years to fully move into, furnish, and settle into a house. Yeah—not me. Instead, for an entire month, my days completely consisted of painting accent walls, finding every covered duct and weak spot I hadn't noticed before buying, and, most of all, trips to and from furniture and housewares stores. HomeGoods, West Elm, Target—you know the drill.

This day, after grabbing yet another bookshelf and catch-all basket, I loaded my purchases into my RV and drove the giant back down the country road.

A few minutes into the drive I passed by an old Methodist church, and a performance by Crystal Lewis and Bryan Duncan I'd once watched with my grandmother popped into my head. As I wound around the country roads, against all car-safety wisdom, I dangerously searched through YouTube for that video. When I finally found it, I listened to it twice. And it led me down a rabbit hole of old hymns, old white crooners, and old Black choirs. No cool points would be acquired on this ride home as I swayed my head to the beat and went down my embarrassingly *old-school* playlist in a moment of concentrated peace. Just me, the one-lane country road, my RV, and my dated music.

After half an hour, when I made the turn back into my driveway, I noticed how autumn had taken over. My home normally looked like something off a Hallmark card, but today the sun was covered by unproductive clouds, the summer heat was leaving with the migrating warblers, and the trees were losing their density. Most of my asphalt was covered in twigs, sap, and leaves.

I parked the vehicle in the garage, pulled out a heavy-duty broom, and started sweeping the driveway. After a few minutes, I realized how, for the last forty minutes or so, my thoughts had been refreshingly detached from my mountain. I had not thought of any ways to engage fans, maintain my image, put out fires, motivate the team, or create anything. I hadn't considered anyone else's opinion, gaze, or narrative. I was content with myself and the music. And the God in the music. I'm sure there were projects to finish and issues to work out, but at this moment, I felt peace, stillness, and oxygen. Unlike the *cold* experience of being by myself on the mountain, I felt a *warm* solitude. Aloneness in the climb feels like neglect and alienation. Aloneness in the valley feels like focused attention. One feels like *I don't matter to anyone.* The other feels like *I'm the only one who matters.*

God was concerned with just me. I was concerned with just us. And my driveway.

No one would care how clean the asphalt was. No new crown would be earned from an immaculate driveway. TikTok would not be interested, and the neighbors would not be impressed. Nothing about the last forty minutes would elevate me in my profession, complete my assignment, or directly push me to my destiny. This valley time would only bring me to awareness of myself and God's closeness.

This moment existing in the valley reminded me of something I couldn't believe I hadn't realized: *I am important to my life.*

You are important to *your* life.

You.

Not the worker, the father, the boss, the queen, or the owner. Just *you*. Son. Daughter.

Dr. Corey Yeager, a renowned marriage and family therapist, said in a men's mental health forum I hosted, "This idea of being OK with who I am . . . is really almost an absent thought for us. I have to be a good dad and good at work. But before I do this, I have to be a good Corey to Corey."

You are important to *your* life.

I'm amazed by how self-centered, self-absorbed, and selfish we can be on the mountain, yet still neglect self. On the mountain, we tend not to give ourselves the maintenance, grace, and humanity we deserve. We don't take the days off we need. We find it hard to forgive ourselves for not winning or not getting the promotion. And we certainly don't sit in the renewing presence of God long enough to be restored. Yes, the God-given assignment is important to my time on earth. The grind is a major factor of life. Other people—their feedback, their patronage, and their favor—matter. But so do I. My intimacy needs, my nutrition, my peace. My feelings, my health, my wholeness.

The Christian life is certainly dutiful and God-centered. There is a sense in all of us that rather than focus on ourselves and our own satisfaction, we should simply focus on God. That is a sound concept, as no agenda is more integral to the fate of the world than God's, and no relationship is more important to our individual destinies than the one we have with Him.

That idea of self-denial for the cause and worship of something bigger is very easily taken to the extreme, though—into self-neglect. More people than we'd like to admit disregard their health, hygiene, sanity, and fashion to prove that nothing else really matters. Every day we must pray that God's love keeps them from going crazy, dying of diabetes, or being musty. I don't know if He always will, but I do know He's perfectly able, so there is hope.

The true, hopeless situation, however, is when "God" gets replaced by "mission" or "assignment." We unreasonably neglect our child-of-God self for the mission. As I write this, I am fasting from dawn to sunset, and I have been painfully hungry since 10:00 a.m. I've been praying, running errands, and enjoying being God's son. I am surprised by how hunger is so loud today, in the valley. In contrast, when I'm climbing, painstakingly working in the studio, I have to be *reminded* by friends to eat at all!

When work is at the center, I neglect my basic needs until my body is screaming. But I've noticed that when God is truly at the center of my life, I take better care of myself. The Spirit leads me in the direction of prosperous health! Positive, optimistic thoughts take the pressure off my mind. I have fewer depression-caused cookie binges. The self-serving things that normally compete for His place in our minds are normally *not* health, sanity, and hygiene. Incredible, right? Yeah, all the self-centered, narcissistic, idol-worshiping thoughts in the world seem to fall short of truly caring about the actual health of our souls and bodies.

One important realization I've had is that filling your desires and meeting your needs are not the same thing.

When we do care about—truly *care* and not just slavishly serve—ourselves, we find out that God is the best thing we can do for *us*. His Word becomes less a manual for how to stay saved and more a manual for how to be whole. And all the quick fixes—sex, drugs, alcohol, and distractions— that we use to shut ourselves up for a night are exposed as weak, impotent, ineffectual, and unwise.

As I swept the driveway, I recognized just how unfamiliar this peace and clarity and *margin* was for me. That day, the Gaithers and Hezekiah Walker were the soundtracks of my arrival in the valley.

I wondered how many times my music was the soundtrack to someone else's arrival in the valley.

Those wonderful listeners of mine would have been enjoying God in a way I hadn't in all those years of creating and promoting and ministering. I never would have considered if Bill Gaither or one of Hezekiah's lead singers was starving on top of their mountain, and I bet none of my listeners would've guessed how frail my soul was either.

I may or may not have shed a very masculine, tough, Southside tear. Just one—like Denzel Washington in *Glory*.

And I thought, *God, please save the man whose climb makes others whole, but who can't participate in wholeness himself! God, save the woman who provides peace without peace!*

As the—again, very strong, adult, and manly—tear fell from my eye, so did a few months of jadedness, unbelief, trauma, and loneliness. My vision had been noticeably compromised by the mountain fog, weakened by the lack of intimacy with God, and cropped by my self-preservation. But now in the valley, feeling like a son again, I had a different view.

Living in the Fullness of Who You Are

I met a professional wrestler once.

Not the Olympic kind. The fun kind. Call it the fake kind if you want. But it was the kind I grew up watching. And no, it wasn't The Rock, who was basically my role model throughout middle school, or else this whole book would have been restructured and called *Too High on the Rock*, or something like that.

To avoid revealing who he was or even helping you narrow it down, I'll keep using "he." And he wasn't "Stone Cold" Steve Austin, either; this guy was a professional wrestler nonetheless. So, the encounter was pretty cool.

I showed up to a star-studded event in Hollywood. It was the kind that, at best, leaves one slot open for a gospel or inspirational artist, and I was honored—and intimidated—to be that night's Jesus moment. Before the event kicked off, some of your favorite music and film stars—and I—lined up at the beginning of a crowded, chaotic red carpet.

These moments always amuse me—for three reasons.

One, I am overwhelmed by the sheer mayhem of stars expecting prompt attention and their publicists (who seem to never be tall) tunneling violently through the crowd of fans. Plus, even more celebrity *hopefuls* (euphemism) looking for star treatment themselves. There is enough entitlement and urgency here to last the world for a year.

Two, I am normally either very familiar and respected by someone or completely off their radar. With every step I take, I vacillate between staff that knows me, reveres my genre, and works to give me the same treatment as Taylor Swift; and staff that has no idea who I am, how to pronounce my name, and can't wait for me to move so they can get back to more important people's business.

Three, I care enough to remember these details and write about them, but compared to the multitude here, I don't think I care much. One more picture. One more interview. A little more shine for my outfit. I don't need it at all.

But this was Hollywood. And I tried my best to shut up and just do as the Hollywoodians do. After the coordinator assigned to me—or maybe just the one who recognized me—protested for my equal civil rights, there I was smiling for the line of photographers.

"Over here!"

"To the right, please!"

"One more over here!" The lenses and lights yelled at me until my publicist-for-the-evening gently pulled me away to my first interview.

I might be stretching a bit here, but as I continued down the line of reporters, the congested red carpet had to have felt like the crowd that almost "crushed" Jesus in Luke 8. You have to numb yourself to the shoulder rubs, the elbows, the dresses, the voracious reporters, and the forceful publicists. But sometimes amid the chaos, you feel a different, more meaningful reach for your attention. I followed the gentle tap on my back to discover a short, stern-looking but surprisingly friendly lady standing beside me.

Now, she certainly wasn't looking for any Luke-8-like healing from any "issue of blood," but she was at least happy to see me. She complimented me on my music and introduced herself as a manager of someone who wanted to meet me. She then directed me to her left, as a striking figure emerged gracefully from the lights and noise. The wrestler was disarmed and intrigued by his normally stoic manager's excitement. So he smiled and asked me for a picture, and we briefly talked about the craziness of the event. Away from the cameras, even though we didn't know each other, we'd found some common ground. There was a moment of normalcy without pretense. It was nice.

Then it was over when I got pulled one way into an interview and he got pulled in another to take more pictures. Now just six feet from each other, we returned to the grind and the character, showing off the most palatable, most inspirational parts of ourselves.

After my interview, I took a couple of steps back toward the red-carpet wall, waiting for the publicist to take me to the next media outlet. At the same time, the wrestler stepped back from his mini-shoot and walked toward me. Now, I am not incredibly aware of the new characters and storylines in professional wrestling—and I haven't been for a decade or two. But I admit I was still a bit enamored by him, if for nothing else, by his Herculean physique and flashy charisma. I'm always honored to "reach over the aisle" and be a peer with someone I never anticipated crossing paths with. There is a shared struggle and secret sport among all entertainers and artists, all influencers and climbers.

So, while I expected a continuation of the reprieve we'd given each other earlier, this interaction was drastically different. This time he stayed in his character. He started saying something about the championship belt he'd just won and how he couldn't stand his archnemesis. The inflated bravado that must have been turned on for the camera *stayed* on. And there I was, lost. I had absolutely *no clue* what he was talking about, and there is probably footage of me standing there with my jaw dropped for a while until I could wrestle it into a nervous smile.

As we continued down the carpet for more interviews, I took that moment with me and examined myself between every redundant question.

I'd like to think that the "character" I choose to be for cameras is not far off from my actual self. I'm still me. Still Jonathan McReynolds. Just likely a more extroverted version. A version that likes hordes of people and isn't insecure in the lights and attention. A version that doesn't get depressed or tempted or discouraged without a Christian answer on hand. It's not that I want to hide those parts. One day, perhaps I'll write a book on how I've combatted depression or my very human résumé of weakness and sin. But most moments don't call for that. What is normally desired by the masses is a public figure's gift, optimism, wisdom, joy for life, and hope.

But that concept was even more exaggerated for this wrestler. No one even knows his real name. And the storyline he presents on TV must be committed to whenever he is near cameras or crowds. Many people don't see these wrestlers as actors but as actual people—colorful caricatures of people—and that act must be maintained everywhere they go. I am expected to have an unlimited well of virtue, but they are expected to have a completely different persona and context from who they might actually be.

We exchanged socials before we parted for the night, and I was grateful that I might have gotten a special forty-five seconds with him that most would never see. But I also was saddened by the weird pressure the climb puts on its inhabitants.

The climb demands a different character out of that wrestler.

The climb demands a different edit of me.

The climb demands a different version of all of us.

And it's not always the version with a redeemable soul or a restorable mind or a healable body.

The IRS, the legal system, and our culture favor these *corporate* entities we leave the house as. Like an LLC protects individuals from getting sued and losing personal assets and gains, our characters and shell versions of ourselves promise to protect us from the scrutiny, drain, and bruises of the climb. But they don't for long, do they?

That shell, that character, that two-dimensional version of yourself is also being "guarded" from love, redemption, understanding, and grace.

A two-dimensional, static, unchanging figure may be necessary to show your kids or your employees or the cameras. But that third dimension, the "you" that was hidden, is coaxed out by time spent in the valley.

The payoff of systematically and routinely climbing down—less of me, more of God—is the extra room I now possess to be more of me in the safety, intimacy, and gentle correction of the valley. What feels like a reduction of the boss, the king, and the creator as you come down your mountain gives way to a refreshing release for you to be the *son* or *daughter* of God.

How different would our generation be if we truly grasped and applied Matthew 19:14, where Jesus said, "Let the little children come to me, and do not hinder them, for the kingdom of heaven belongs to such as these"? Children, like everyone else, flocked to Him, but the well-intentioned disciples felt kids were too insignificant to waste Jesus' time. Jesus, in turn, rebuked the disciples, as that trusting, wide-eyed, ingenuous child is what He appreciates inside of every believer.

Perhaps the carnality of the world and the restrictive piety of our religious experiences have made us believe we must be masked in the presence of God and save our recklessness for more unsafe places, but time in the valley challenges that myth. The disciples who tried to shoo the kids away were wrong then, and the part of you that starves the child of God in you is wrong now.

The weird, the awkward, the hurt, the disappointed, the mistake-prone, the sinful, the bitter—all are allowed to come out in the valley. While we are representing ourselves, our businesses, and our faith, some of that isn't allowed. We often must keep a smile, resolve, and restraint for the sake of the job. But in the valley, you can express who you truly are. There is censorship and restraint on the mountain, but I am learning to enjoy just how much of me God can take. I underestimated how many doubts, how many fears, how many questions, and how much uncertainty He allows me before I get whupped on the butt. The climb doesn't allow it, and those mountain principles bleed into my religious framework too. Since the fans, the saints, and even some loved ones couldn't handle it, I assumed God couldn't either.

The valley will distinguish God from God's people for you.

The valley will highlight the relationship He wants. Even when it's gotten lost inside of religion.

And most of all, sinking into the valley, being honest with God—brutally honest about my sins, my temptations, my fears, my frustrations, my frustrations with Him—showed me the work I needed to do on me.

To allow yourself to be human in the valley is to know who needs to be crucified daily.

Any redemption for the wrestler would have to be written in the script by the mere human behind fashioning the plot lines. But only the man or woman *underneath* the costume could participate in any *divine* benefit. If I live from the mountain, based on that singular mountain's rules and expectations, existing as the primarily two-dimensional, flat character I must be for other people's sake, I will never appreciate the fluidity, goodness, mercy, peace, joy, grace, and even *other assignments* meant for the three-dimensional son or daughter God created.

> We [wrongfully] become our assignment . . . [A]lways stay a child of God so you can do whatever you're supposed to do at the time.
>
> —Tye Tribbett, pastor and legendary gospel artist[1]

Greatness Versus Goodness

In addition to being able to live three-dimensionally in the valley, two more things tend to happen there. They are potent, pivotal, and yet often overlooked spiritual disciplines. They scream less of me and more of God.

I'm talking about fasting and reading the Word.

They are incredible practices to accompany stillness and prayer.

My childhood church may have been a little pretentious to some and folksy to others. It was lodged in the middle of a Southside neighborhood that—now that I think about it—had a little education and luxury but its fair share of ignorance and ratchetness too. I only say this because I really don't know if some of the methods they taught us were orthodox standards, but they worked for us.

For instance, during a fast, we were taught to pray and think of God every time we felt hungry. Any hunger pang, any stomach growl, any time we got a whiff of someone else's fries, we were to pray and think about Jesus. Read a scripture. Study something. Connect our bodily protests to intentional focus on God. Practical, right?

Well, one day during my fast, I was scrolling on my phone, looking for something to post to pass the hungry time. And the devil entered my phone in the form of an Uber Eats notification and caused me to trail off for a good fifteen seconds about what I would eat . . . if I could eat. I eventually caught myself and identified that tangent as a bodily protest. And just like I was taught, I turned my attention God-ward and casually muttered, "Thank you, Lord, for the great calling on my life." The prayer was rather hasty, but it did send me down a rather pensive rabbit hole.

I heard myself say "great."

And when I said "great," I meant *impactful*—reaching a lot of people, 95 percent of whom I'll never know. I meant greatness in the form of a statue or portrait or billboard. Greatness that extends beyond my inner circle and beyond my family. Greatness that garners followers and wealth and celebrity. I meant greatness that would be on display for all the world to see.

I knew this mountain was given to me by God, and to climb it would eventually result in greatness. Therefore, was it not greatness, *that* kind of greatness, God called me to?

And if God gave me this mountain to climb, I'm sure I could find plenty of scriptures that would support the climb to greatness and encourage me along the way.

Surprisingly, I couldn't find that many.

No, seriously. Look for yourself. The type of greatness we post about and trend for and fawn over is not emphasized nearly as much in the teachings of Christ, nor Moses, nor Solomon, nor Paul, nor anyone in Scripture for that matter.

God challenges us to be fruitful. He endorsed David, enlightened Solomon, and backed a few other characters who had great impact on Israel's narrative. He promised Abraham his obedience would "make [his] name great" (Genesis 12:2). Yes, Jesus prophesied that the works believers do after he returns to the Father will be even "greater" than his own. Paul encouraged the greatness of the up-and-coming church leaders, but it's not the opulent, comfortable greatness we'd shoot for now.

As important as culture makes royalty, C-level executives, superstars, and those striving for success, the Bible does not emphasize that type of greatness at all. There isn't a separate manual for the believers perched high on their mountains. Celebrities may get a special seat in church, but they don't get a special chapter on how to win under the pressure of constant scrutiny.

Recognizing this generation's grind, climb, and win culture, and feeling compelled to engage and inspire that generation, maybe today's preachers have no choice but to key in on a smaller subset of scriptures or use a wee bit of eisegesis to squeak out another sermon. In my opinion, the Scripture-lite motivational messages that pervade our generation of churches are in direct correlation to a generation that emphasizes a type of *greatness* the Bible doesn't.

Let's be honest. We climb to accomplish greatness. We climb for our kids to accomplish greatness. Trophy, status, promotion, credential greatness.

But the Bible, our manual on life and humanity, emphasizes a different set of prizes. A different focus—a different locus. It's generosity and servitude. It's long-suffering, patience, and devotion. It's taking care of your family before you even think about taking care of your church. It's fidelity, attention, and proper prioritization of your faith, your family, and your own soul's prosperity. This is called *goodness*.

Goodness. Good deeds. Good walk. Good talk. Good living. *Goodness.*

God obviously has not called us all to be famous or CEOs or even parents, but He has called everyone to goodness. It is a primary Christian objective, not to climb to the highest heights of business or athletics, but to shine with goodness.

So let's be good as we focus on being great, right? Not quite that easy.

If it were, the landscape of church and politics would be quite different. Our movie stars wouldn't end up overdosing on drugs so much. First families wouldn't produce so many angry and neglected children. Entertainers could withstand the temptations on the climb. I would have had a much less dramatic life.

In our culture, we are watching every day how the demands of greatness and the pursuit of it come at the cost of goodness. Building a megachurch is "great." Prioritizing family and your own peace is "good." And sometimes—very often—those pursuits oppose each other. Burying your head in the computer might preclude you from burying your head in the Good Book. The self-absorption it takes to create amazing album after album, produce book after book, market your new business, or become the best lawyer in the city is inimical to the generosity, patience, and neighbor-mindedness God spends way more time challenging us to show.

After my epiphany in the driveway, I did my best to stay in a valley mindset. A few days later, I sat at home, circulating from my piano, to ESPN, to staring blankly at the woods behind my house. And from this view, I resolved that the tougher chore and the bigger honor would be being known as a good man rather than a "great" one. Obviously, in a perfect world, I would be both. But I feel like I heard God—and am hearing God more and more—asking me to rest in cultivating my goodness rather than sacrificing it for greatness.

Shrewdly stewarding my gifts, talents, money, and network should not run in opposition to treating people well, caring for my soul, and committing to my relationship with God. So often, the extra strides up into the mountain mindset for *greatness's* sake cross that line. The challenge for the climber then becomes committing to the *low life*—the humble, modest, lawful, goodness-cultivating life low in the valley—even more than they commit to elevating their work and mission.

In God's hands, a faithful, natural bend toward goodness just might lead to that billboard-type greatness. Think Joseph, David, and many of the pastors you know. Their faith, their discipline, and their stewarding of God's gifts led to prominence. But once this "greatness" comes into the equation, it is up to the climber to keep it from devouring every morsel of integrity, peace, and joy they have! This type of greatness doesn't naturally lead to goodness. There are plenty of traps, snares, frustrations, and pressures that will attempt to snuff out a queen, a boss, a dad, and a superstar pastor's *goodness*.

According to the Beatitudes of Matthew 5, the lowly and not-so-*great* have a much less encumbered path to the Kingdom of God. Their entrance into heaven is much wider than the rich man's chances.

The Gospels are full of instances where the lowly and hated and marginalized gave up careers, threw down their fishing nets, overcame complacency and illness, and used their last to appreciate, glean from, and follow Jesus.

The richer, more elevated, "great" guys, naturally, had a lot more questions. Poverty can be an impediment to a lot of things, but wealth, fame, and greatness are very often the biggest enemies of good.

OK, I may need a break. I was fasting at the beginning of this chapter, and I'm still fasting now. And I'm having those food-related thoughts again.

We've already established how much of a nerd and over-thinker I've been since birth, right? I remember, very clearly, moments when things didn't make logical sense to me. Like the one day I was sitting at my grandmother's table for breakfast—wonderful, wonderful breakfast. Mmmm . . . food.

Sorry.

We church kids had a standard prayer we'd say before we ate. You've heard it and probably have said it.

God is great, God is good
Let us thank him for our food.

It's a simple, beautiful prayer that no one has had a problem with in probably centuries.

But it bothered me!

I mean, obviously, the writer of this poem was trying his best to eke out a rhyme with "good" and "food." They must have used their eyes to rhyme rather than their ears back then.

But a rhyme at what cost?!

Why diminish God from "great" to "good" in one line?!

How did God start off amazing to you but then, after one comma, you downgrade him to just decent?! If anything, I'd expect our praises to *rise* in intensity and appreciation. From "good" to "great." But perhaps God knew it'd bother me and that, one day, He'd get me off my overachieving mountain and into His marvelous valley and prove the poet was wiser than we could've ever imagined.

From God's perspective, "good" may be better than "great."

The creation story of Genesis 1 shows God creating light and calling it *good*. Day and night, *good*. Animals, *good*. Plants, *good*. People, well, you know . . . he didn't say *good* in quite the same manner. But I digress. My point here is God's version of "good" has outclassed and outlasted every iteration of humanity's idea of "great."

From the mountain, the thin air will have you feeling that your climb into greatness is getting you *closer* to God and self-actualization.

But this less glorious, yet much more oxygenated, clearer view from the valley shows me I never had to work like this to reach Him. All that sacrifice. All those degrees. All that stressing. All those standard mountain issues that led to sinful behavior, compromise, and high blood pressure. Just to find out that it all falls short of being a *good* child of a *good* God.

So our challenge in life is not simply to be "great," make a name for ourselves, earn some cool accolades, and raise kid celebrities. Our challenge is to pursue and hold on to the "good" even as the earthly stakes get higher and our name becomes great on its own. Our challenge is to balance the great demands of the mountain with a "lower life" in the valley of sonship or daughterhood, God's presence, and goodness.

CHAPTER 8

PLAN A BETTER WAY UP

A long time ago, I was twenty-four or twenty-five, beginning to travel, just my guitar and me, performing, or as some Christians prefer to call it, *ministering* around the country.

I had begun to master the two-song, ten-minute set launched by an improvised intro to neutralize the crowd. Sometimes it was traditional and churchy; other times it was R&B and youthful. Then came my first popular song, "No Gray." Make sure they hear the chorus clearly. Scat. Smile at the end. Transition with a mini-sermon from the idea of God's standard of holiness to his standard of grace and unconditional love. Sing "Lovin' Me" with the church-approved ad-libs at the end. Reprise if warranted. Bow out humbly. Sit uncomfortably back in my seat. Head out five minutes before the event or service ends. Unwrap some CDs and find a Sharpie. Sit there awkwardly until people patronize the table. Receive love, sign autograph, take a picture. Accept phone numbers from women, or their mothers on their behalf, sign, take a picture. Keep a paralyzed smile through criticism and finger-wagging, sign, take a picture. Try not to leave a big black Sharpie mark on their good clothes when they hug you. Thank the pastor. Back to the hotel.

I had grown accustomed to this rhythm. It had become a blur. I know I was breathing and probably looking very natural and confident while I did my job, but each breath was shallow. For five hours, I hadn't really inhaled or exhaled. I hadn't truly taken the performance, the response, and the post-show interactions all the way in.

I was more of a posable action figure that whole time than a human being. Doing what needed to be done. Conveying the message that God gave me. Numbing myself to the unpredictable responses of people. In those moments, I don't think I was very present, or I would've screamed more as the nerdy introvert inside was drowning in a flood of direct human contact. I also might have cussed someone out a few times, as some of the things that were said to me were more ridiculous than you could ever imagine. Or perhaps I would've just cried at the sheer impact I seemed to be making.

But I wasn't present.

In these early years I visited Los Angeles, the land of hills and valleys, and pulled up to a large church for an absolutely legendary gospel singer's conference. It was an honor to have one of the biggest names in our industry endorsing and having me on her program. I don't even remember if I had been paid very much to come, or anything at all. It was likely just a free plane ticket and hotel room and enough per diem to buy food. Back then, ministering/performing was about the honor, the exposure, and the opportunity, so I gladly obliged.

This gospel singer's conferences were likely fiery and charismatic at night, but I was called in for the lighter, less energetic day sessions. I walked in to a sparsely attended section that had been walled off for the afternoon. Perhaps one hundred people woozily nodded to whatever the speaker was talking about, leaving a quiet hum of *amens* smattering across the room. I must have been late, because after a few minutes the legend herself began to emcee and rile up the crowd a bit as she invited me up to the stage.

I plugged in my guitar and rushed to the mic as soon as possible to mitigate the awkward silence—like always. I said my hellos, spoke honorably of the legend, smiled, and strummed a quiet G-chord just to make sure the guitar was working. I looked around and noticed the crowd was kind of older and churchy and full of women. So I chose a certain icebreaker that I felt was appropriate and started the song.

This sounds cocky, but sometimes after singing with the guitar for five seconds, the ladies in the audience would start losing it a little bit. Shrieks and "hmmms" and "alrights" would fill the room, but if I could maintain my composure, more attention would be drawn to the convicting lyrics of the song. And as a songwriter first, that's what mattered the most. If by the time I got to the second verse, the church had an audible hum of people—even the guys—commenting under their breath or to one another, I knew things were going well. After the second chorus, I'd scat a little bit. By then, the musical exhibition would have reached a climax and I'd be home free.

Well, things were going well, and sure enough, as I approached the scat section, people were already adequately intrigued and blessed by the words. I knew it'd be icing on the cake.

Two bars in, though, the gospel legend who had invited me stood up from her front-row seat and walked toward the stage. Loudly encouraging and hyping me up like only a lady from a Black, Pentecostal church could, she came to the edge of the stage, right in front of the mic stand and my feet, and slapped a few twenty-dollar bills onto the platform. Though this was uncommon at my childhood church, it wasn't uncommon in a lot of churches around the country. When a congregant feels like the preacher or singer is really bringing it and blessing their lives, it is not abnormal for them to run to the stage with a bill or two to "sow" into that man or woman of God.

It was a first for me, though, especially since my music doesn't sound like the normal soundtrack for that kind of Pentecostal charismatic environment, but I maintained pace and kept going. After taking her moment, she motioned to the rest of the crowd to follow suit.

This is when it got weird.

She looked at me like a neighborhood "big mama" and firmly commanded that I "keep singing." In a matter of seconds, at least half of that audience was rushing to the stage and dropping money at my feet. I'm sure there is a very pious, traditional, solemn, or bridled way to do this, but this was not that. I was young and sheltered, and the moment was flying by so fast that I know my memory is probably making this worse than it was. But I recall a little bit of a panty-throwing vibe going on.

A little Elvis-y.

A little "rake-it-up, rake-it-up" stripper energy.

And her repeated instruction to "keep singing" was not helping the situation.

After the smoke cleared and everyone gleefully jogged back to their seat, high-fiving on the way, I walked off the stage—feeling naked.

What was that?! I thought.

I guess I knew I had succeeded and, from the looks of it, earned a thousand bucks to boot. But I had no frame of reference or context for what had just happened.

To add to the head-scratching, shortly after the program moved on, that gospel legend, proud of me and that moment, came up to me with gratitude and advice.

"Don't change," she said.

That's it.

What on earth did that mean?! Don't change what? My musical approach? My haircut? My gospel-stripping ways? What?

Looking back, a decade of high highs and low lows later, I bet she probably meant something like, "Don't let the mountain change you."

"Don't lose heart when your input doesn't always match the output."

"Don't get too high in your ambitions and progress that you spend less time with God."

"Don't let experiences like old ladies running up to the stage with twenty-dollar bills change your idea of success."

"Don't let this naked, lonely feeling make you grow cold."

Often, we are not precisely warned about the dangers on the mountain. We are given quick motivational tags without any real explanation of what's to come. In my world of moral scrutiny and pious projection, the red line is sin. The red line is public exposure of the sin. But no one speaks much to those sneaky, standard mountain issues that lead to it.

That's what this book is for.

There will be days that shift you into a different level of climb. Moments that demand you get a bit more absorbed in your mission. Events that radically shift your idea of what success is, how much you need it, and how much you're expected to have it. And if you haven't prepared in the valley, you will burn out and maybe even die on the mountain.

The climb is a conscious choice, but the altitude sneaks up on you!

We don't normally consciously say yes to the entire journey. We aren't able to knowledgeably climb with complete readiness for what's to come. Instead, we say yes incrementally, often unaware of how far that yes will take us before the next opportunity to say no.

We don't say yes to motherhood or fatherhood nearly as consciously as we say yes to unprotected sex.

We don't say yes to fame as consciously as we say yes to practice, rehearsal, and excellence in our craft.

We don't say yes to every risk, sacrifice, and hour spent struggling nearly as deliberately as we say yes to avoiding getting a "regular" job.

I didn't say yes to being a successful, working, traveling, autograph-signing artist as consciously as I said yes to representing myself well and trying not to be bad at things.

I had no clue how to prepare for the way up.

But now I know better. You do too. So, let's prepare better.

Eat! Eat!

Eat as much as you can.
—Alpenglow Expeditions, mountain guides[1]

It should not surprise you that most of the weight professional mountain climbers carry in their packs comes from food. The food operation for a climber is essential. For big climbs up Everest, there are camps set up at different levels of the mountain not only for climbers to get used to the cold but also to eat!

And boy, do they eat!

Because of the strenuous exercise of climbing mountains, professional climbers can consume eight to ten thousand calories a day. That is crazy because, according to my cereal box, we regular humans need only two thousand calories a day. As professional climbers leave the relatively good, cooked meals of each camp, the constant intake of calories keeps them going.

While many people feel that humans were *made* to grind and work hard and always climb, our bodies and minds show that the grind is constantly operating at our highest level of productivity, intensity, and strategy. The climb takes from us! It utilizes what we have consumed to fuel itself and doesn't give it back. It will burn the fat and muscle off our bones if we don't continue eating—and eating in extraordinary fashion.

Fruits, vegetables, protein, and carbs are necessary for human life regardless, but on your mountain, you're going to need a steady, elevated diet of spiritual food as well.

These days, I tend to lose about ten pounds of body weight on long tours and a few more while working on an album. I also tend to gain it all back when it's over. But there is so much more loss aside from the physical calories. I lose a lot of emotional mass navigating social media, fighting with Uncle Algorithm, and enduring the land mines of the many ignorant, egocentric users. I burn a year's worth of mental calories doing cartwheels trying to meet a deadline, choreograph a performance, or rearrange a set to accommodate someone's request. My stomach oddly growls after hearing, holding my breath, and smiling through some of the most eye-roll-worthy interactions with believers and leaders around the world. Oh, the toll it all takes on the way I understand, desire, and trust God!

I burned out climbing to the summit because I was using more mental and spiritual calories than I was consuming.

It wasn't always like that. I remember days when the ratio wasn't quite as bad.

When I began making music in my dorm room, I was well fed. I attended church twice a week. There was no pressure or public responsibility; therefore less energy was expended. Like most college kids who grew up going to church, I dabbled in both the profound and the ridiculous corners of Christian YouTube and constantly reconciled my African History class with biblical accounts.

When my career launched in 2011, I still regularly attended a couple of churches, including my childhood church, where I'd not only eat but serve. And we already know how serving—the non-climbing, taking-the-garbage-out kind—can keep you nourished in the valley. I'd zip from playing the organ, to installing new mics and sound equipment, to shoveling snow, to supervising some of the little kids for a while, to singing in a baby's ear to get him to quiet down during the sermon, to taking notes on the sage wisdom of my pastor. I ate a lot of good food.

As my career began to gain some momentum, I found myself in radio interview after TV interview, being asked for insight and encouragement for the listeners. I felt underqualified—spiritually and biblically—to be given such a platform that was only partially musical. In

Christian culture, musical gifts typically morph into ministerial responsibilities, which is dangerous for the artists and detrimental to the Church long term, but that's for another book. To catch up to this newly bestowed honor I had, I went to school. So, from 2013–2015, I earned a master's in biblical studies from Moody Theological Seminary. I honestly didn't go to claim that cool credential. I went to eat.

During the next few years, a couple more albums were released, there were more TV appearances, more preaching (yes, preaching—I was surprised too), more travel, more guitars on my back, more pressure to demonstrate a public-approved image of *godliness*, and even a song called "Pressure." I began burning more spiritual, inspirational, and essential calories than I ate. I still had plenty of reserves, though, and wasn't tired or burned out, so I kept climbing higher and higher up the mountain. And you already know where that left me. The table was spread down in the Jerusalem valley but not so much up on the wild mountain.

While we sit in the valley, preparing to go back on the road, back to the grind, and back to the hustle and bustle, we must consider what we will need to eat when we're up on the mountain. The valley is a place of both restoration and preparation. The valley is where we return to our healthy weight and where we pack the food we know we will need on our journey back up.

So, let's get started with the meal prep.

Meal Prep

Professional climbers, the ones who scale Everest, Denali, and Kilimanjaro, consume calorie-dense *proteins* and *fats* as they begin their trek. We're talking fish, beans, chicken breasts, lean beef, eggs, milk, and peanut butter. These calories will become useful down (up) the road when every step becomes strenuous and food is sparse. The proteins and fats humans regularly consume are major factors that determine our physique, our body type, and our muscle. Proteins break down into amino acids that are the building blocks of our tissues. Plus, they are the final and primary resource for energy and for resolve. Fats help proteins do their job. They store energy, insulate us, and offer protection for our vital organs. Your protein and fat content are the biggest determinants of how long you can go in the gym and how high you can go on your mountain. As professional climbers prepare for their ascent, showing up properly packed with proteins and fats—in their bodies and in their bags—is a must!

Similarly, *spiritual* and *theological* proteins and healthy fats build, shape, and strengthen us as sons and daughters as we arrive at the beginning of the climb. In 1 Corinthians 3:2, Paul referred to this type of necessary food as the "milk" and "meat" of revelation, discipline, and insight. The Corinthians' inability, in his eyes, to digest or even hunger for more grown-up forms of protein and fat was an indicator of the *shape* their faith and hearts were in.

This kind of food—the meat and milk, the protein and fat—is mostly found in the slow, intentional, and still moments in God's presence. It's where you give space for God to download ideas, strategies, plans, and a deep understanding of who you are in Him. The message may come through a sermon or through reading, but the most important element is that *you* digest it and let it become a building block of who you are. Fresh off a fast, Scripture reading, stillness, or practiced intimacy with God, our minds often become full of revelation and insight needed for the climb. Consuming this type of food in the valley changes you and prepares you to not be so eaten at the core and famished into frailty on the mountain.

When I am in the valley, I am reminded of our God-given muscle as sons or daughters of the Most High. We have the authority and the green light to make moves, expand the Kingdom, make money, and "occupy till [the Master comes]" (Luke 19:13 KJV). That bit of protein gives me strength and is needed in abundance during the climb.

In the valley, I am reminded of the God-given gifts I've been afforded and my responsibility to turn the five talents of gold the Master gave me into ten (referring to the parable of the ten minas in Luke 19). I have been gifted certain talents, resources, and strengths that aid me in accomplishing in this life. They make my mountain mindset successful in the public sphere. When I work hard and work smart, good things happen because of the power and giftings God has given me. Same for you. I realize my value despite the gifts, personality traits, and opportunities I *do not*—and *may never*—have. No matter how high I climb into the clouds, some things aren't meant for me to do, and some things certainly aren't meant for me to do alone. Yummm . . . that protein-filled reminder, that fatty truth, shapes me.

"Who is God?" "Who are you?" Those are simple three-word questions with the most complicated, powerful, and heavy answers. To properly prepare for the climb, we must make sure that we have prepped and packed sufficient answers to those questions. Those protein-, fat-, and calorie-dense answers define the shape and strength of your faith as you begin to climb.

But as mountaineers get higher, in addition to the protein and fat, they begin to rely heavily on another type of food. This fare is lighter to carry than, say, steak and potatoes, and it breaks down and digests much more easily. Higher altitudes lack water and oxygen to power the body's digestive system. The heavy steak and potatoes can cause nausea up there, but this other variety of nutrition is made up of smaller molecules that absorb quickly—like as soon as a spoonful lands in your mouth.

I'm talking about carbs. Carbohydrates. Oats, energy bars, bananas, and even candy; whether it burns slow like oatmeal or fast like Starburst, carbs give you what you need before you tap into your fat reserves.

For us metaphorical climbers, part of our meal prep includes quick bursts of inspiration, reframing, and energy for the grueling moments we can now anticipate. I have talked about standard mountain issues like loneliness, intimacy, and lack. We also know that heartache, discouragement, and disappointment can spring from those issues. Even for the saved. Even for the believing. Even for the full of faith. We need our carbs as we ascend to remind us we're OK and that this mountain is not our home.

If you ever steal and hack into my phone, you will see a note called "For Depression." Depression is, unfortunately, one of the frequent symptoms of my climb. My mountain mindset presents as manic-like episodes where I am highly focused, productive, and motivated by delusions of grandeur. I feel like a warrior, a king, a beast. But somewhere along the way, this energy dips low into inadequacy, anxiety, and delusions of imposter syndrome.

"For Depression" reads like a list of mini-letters from in-the-valley me to the depressed version of me and consists of responses to common triggers. They come in the form of Scripture, photos, and videos. They evidence my good life, good character, and right standing with God (grace). They feature proof of the existence of a lovable, valuable, and joyful version of me for the times when I can't fathom that guy. This reminds me who is in my corner and who still thinks I'm pretty awesome. Photos of Uncle Cessie's look of approval. Or my niece proudly accepting an award on my behalf. Or my nephew and I surprising each other on the same morning show as he promoted his movie and I promoted my album. I even include a link to that video of when Berklee's Jonathan McReynolds Ensemble had a concert, and I hid in the back to watch. And the link of the video of me directing my own class at Columbia College. And the link of my then-still-living grandmother briefly snapping back from dementia as she proudly watched me sneak some of her favorite old-school hymns into my concert.

Wow. Praise break. God has been so good.

Just typing that, reliving those memories and engaging those reminders, made me quite grateful and emotional. I had a tough time getting through that paragraph.

When you feel yourself succumbing to the thin air and strenuous work of the mountain, rely on these energy bars of faith, gratitude, reflection, and inspiration. What can this look like for you? Nuggets from the Word of God? Screenshots of encouraging text messages from others? Photos of your favorite people who love and believe in you? Quotes from books that inspire and energize you?

If you happen to encounter some of that mountain-induced depression, chew on a handful of perspective to address it like I did with the "proofs" of love and affirmation in my life. Climb-distorted faith? Munch on a dose of Scripture to strengthen your true identity. Doubt as to your direction? Unwrap a moment from your past where God was surely protecting, providing, or making a way. Daily, twice a day, eight times a day, prepare snacks *from* the valley to keep you grounded, going, and focused.

> *I need a song that will keep my*
> *mind stayed on Him.*[2]

I love stimulating thought, intense conversation, and deep music. I challenge my listeners to lean into the lyrics as much as I do. I put a lot of work into fine-tuning every line so that it speaks truth to power. My songs are written with nutrient-dense heartiness on purpose. I'll never forget when Bishop Hezekiah Walker, the legendary and decorated choir leader and pastor from New York, said after I performed a set, "In a world where a lot of us are encouraged to give the people candy, you cook them vegetables." I felt validated in that moment for all the nerdy, overly analytical, and obsessive moments in the studio.

I've gotten older, though, and I've obviously hit some rough high points on my mountain. And now I know, sometimes we just need candy! Or at least crackers. Those carbs—those easy-to-digest, easy-to-prepare snacks—serve a major purpose for a climber.

In an effort to make my sets easier to digest, I often add a little bit of nostalgia—some of the hymns or nursery rhymes I grew up with. And while it may seem corny on paper, I must admit that few moments on tour resonate quite like when I throw "Yes, Jesus Loves Me" into a particular song. It's not a meaty phrase. It's a song taught to four-year-old children. No one is getting asked to a conference just to preach or sing that! But that simple truth—God's unconditional love for us—is like a Snickers to a tired and starving climber when the sun is starting to go down.

As a matter of fact, music is a light, easily digestible snack that can help keep us energized and inspired on the mountain.

Pack some music! It isn't heavy, you can bring a lot of it, and, if you choose your playlists well, they will overflow with the digestible reminders and spiritual nutrition that you need. Pick songs that will keep your mind stayed on God. Music is used as a soundtrack for everything. But for the believer on the mountain, this very light but possibly nutrition-packed meal can keep us energized, grateful, and connected to the valley.

Songs, scriptures, notes from a "valley-er" self, quotes from past sermons—how creative can you get with your meal prep? People create vision boards at the beginning of the year. How can you make sure it's sufficient for use beyond January? Have at your immediate disposal clips of sermons or inspirational interviews that God led you to.

We now know that spiritual and soul-keeping food will be slim pickings on the mountain. Your schedule may preclude your attendance at church gatherings. It shouldn't, but you know it may. Your focus on the kids may have you feeling quite untended to. A stressful season at work may pull on all your reserves of joy and peace. So, what God has shown you in the valley must be recorded, kept, prepped, and packed for future remembrance, future maintenance, and future sustenance on the mountain.

Mark Your Trail

My process down the mountain took months. I was working against a career that was steadily growing and a personal life that was still *life-ing.* I still had to tour. I still had to host. I endured some more bad news. Some more death. I still had to perform at a high level. Still took care of things. That steady dose of responsibility and hardship made it more difficult to drop the ego, gratefully recall the broken yet divine road that had gotten me here, broaden my view of life and people, and trust God enough to be still and pray. Therefore, that climb down was exhausting, scary, and not always straightforward.

The payoff in the valley—proof that there was a valley of sonship for me—was absolutely worth it, but I don't ever want to have to endure such a sharp U-turn again. I don't ever want to be so stuck on the mountain that it hurts to get back home. If we want to be the bosses, the kings and queens, the parents, and the achievers we feel called to be, we *will* find ourselves back to being driven by a mountain mindset. We weren't created to live on the summit nor frolic without labor in the valley for the rest of our lives. It's a balancing act.

We need to make sure we know how to get back down to the valley more efficiently.

The steps outlined a couple of chapters ago are a potential panacea for everyone stuck on the slopes, but the time and force it takes could be lessened if we paid a little more attention to what gets us up there in the first place. This requires taking note of the moments that contradict the steps that brought you down to the valley.

I want to admit something.

Do you remember that valley moment I had while sweeping the driveway? When I had spent an hour or so listening to nostalgic music, worshiping, talking to God, and talking to myself? Well, I wasn't totally forthright with what happened even in that moment. I may have done better the next day, but in the *minutes* following that moment, I found myself ascending again.

I sat there in the epiphany and, just like with all the previous epiphanies I'd had before, I thought about how much it would inspire and impact others. It had only been five minutes! If the valley was water and I was a sponge, I'd still be mostly dry. Yet I was already thinking of how to release that message to the public. *How do I say it? How will people react? How well will the Instagram algorithm distribute it? Do I look unkempt in this hoodie? What view shows the least information about where I live—still keeping the post-worthy trees in the background?*

I touched the valley and, that quickly, started climbing again so I could be the one to tell everyone about it.

All that stillness was lost.

The absolute *opposite* of the point. The opposite of the valley.

There I was. Once again the main character, hyper-focused on my post, my life, and its value to the world. Dipping into God's résumé only to find the right authentic-sounding words to craft the message. Thrusting myself back into social media, the Land of Ego, for scrutiny, obsessing over engagement numbers and wondering if I needed to be doing something more "productive" or profitable.

After posting my moment, I was still in a good mood, but my heart was beating a little faster. I lost a little interest in sweeping the driveway, as monitoring likes and comments seemed more satisfying. Even though my post was about me momentarily escaping the pressure, the gaze, and the weight of what I do, I immediately reengaged with that weight to produce and upload it. An authentic valley experience choked by the mountain mindset in a mountainous culture.

I felt like a drug addict desperate for public visibility, or a fraud talking about a moment I barely was present in, or, at the very least, a complete head case hooked on attention. Just as I was starting to feel loved, I prematurely restarted the climb, and now I was feeling unlovable again. I caught myself, though. And rather than continue to beat myself up, I *marked my trail*.

I noted where ego came in. I recognized how and when I wanted to be seen or noticed or applauded or respected, or all those things. I noticed how I prioritized the people's peace over my own and the people's good graces over God's. I saw where I moved from son to artist. From being to doing. From God-given status to self-ordained God-esque assignment.

No one was in this driveway, but I was embarrassed.

I repented to God. I also apologized to myself. That sacred space was for me too.

After we have enjoyed the presence, the intimacy of God in worship, prayer, and general peace and joy, we must be aware of the moments we turn back upward and reengage the climb. Watch out for when you reverse the humbling steps down—quieting ego, remembering God's résumé, "calling your nephew," and stillness—and start to head up. Watch for the moments when your title and responsibility take over your day.

Seasons of climbing are necessary in life, but make sure you know how you got up there! That trail upward reveals the quickest way back down. After too long, too many gigs, too many meetings, too much applause, and too much criticism, we have no clue why we are cold and losing breath up high on a cliff. Some of it wasn't even necessary. Some of those worries were unfounded. Some of those moments stirred up a lot of fear but had little real effect on the end result. Some of those people—and their opinions—didn't matter. But it all pushed us up and away from the valley, up and away from being a daughter or son of God.

As you climb, be aware of and sensitive to the altitude. Pay attention to the moments that put your assignment, career, and titles at the center of everything, and move God to the perimeter. When we mark our trail, we know a little bit better what to address in our hearts and minds, and we can come down more efficiently.

On the Mountain, but Not of the Mountain

Sheila E. just texted me.

Yeah, *that* Sheila E. One of the most famous drummers, musicians, and performers of all time.

She said she was proud of me and, among other things, she admonished me to "commit to fostering a harmonious balance as you pursue your aspirations. I firmly believe that your well-being is paramount on this path to greatness."

How did she know that, for this season, I've truly been studying and applying and writing about this great balance that all who aspire to be "great" should explore? I think she pegged me as a climber, like I've pegged you as one. She knows that while I strive for great things, great feats, great accolades, and great impact, I tend to neglect myself and the important things in life. I neglect my well-being. I neglect the valley of God's presence and fathering, rest, and nutrition. I have found it hard to strike that "harmonious balance" from week to week.

That may be the most important balance we will learn in this life.

We *will* be on the mountain. We will take time working, progressing, attempting to obtain, retain, and maintain. We will lock in, grind, hustle, study, and compete. We will win some and we will lose some. Yes, we will be *on* the mountain, but we don't have to be *of* it. We don't have to be defined by it. We don't have to center our entire lives around it. And we are better off, with fuller lives, and maybe even with more fuel to achieve greatness, if we keep the mountain in its proper place.

I forgot to mention that my response to Sheila E.'s message had "mountain mindset" written all over it. She said "congratulations," and my internal response was "for what?!"

See, a couple of nights before, while most people would say I was blessed to have been nominated for a Grammy, I was dejected because I fell short of winning. Her congratulations were like salt crystals to a new wound. I had let myself down. I had climbed and climbed and gotten so close to that second Grammy, I could almost taste it. And there's nothing quite like the taste of metal ten thousand feet up in the clouds.

But her response was the key to it all: "[Congratulations] for just being you."

Perhaps I missed the A-plus and fell short with the end-of-the-year numbers. But that success or failure is disconnected from the core of who I am—who you are. Mountain successes should only inflate you to a point. And failures should have a limit on how much they can bring you down. The best and worst you can be will always be a child of God. And no matter how long you've been up in the clouds, bossing and queening and managing, the valley will always exist for you.

Provided you exist for the valley.

CHAPTER 9

STAY ANCHORED TO THE VALLEY

OK, so this weird thing has been happening to me lately. According to all my friends, I don't drink enough water. That part isn't new. They've told me that repeatedly over the years, but I'd simply scoff at their censure and tell them of the "many" bottles I had drunk over a two- or three-day span. I could normally recall starting at least four bottles, though I don't know if I actually finished them. I'd assume that if I could remember four, I probably forgot seven.

The lies we tell ourselves.

My friends are right. I really don't drink enough water. And now I can tell, because there are times when I finally pick up a bottle and raise it to my lips, and my body kind of goes crazy. Something within me gets ravenous and intense. My hands get a little shaky, my throat pops out of my mouth, and my lips grip the bottle as if I had been stranded in the desert for a week. I guzzle the liquid in a few seconds, and a tithe of it almost always ends up on my beard and shirt.

Our bodies are comprised of mostly water—up to 75 percent of our bodies, somehow, is well-organized water. It's essential for cellular homeostasis and life. Water regulates body temperature, maintains our muscles, lubricates joints, prevents constipation, flushes out waste products, carries nutrients to our cells, and protects our organs and tissues.[1]

We need water.

But when I refuse to provide my body with what it needs, it slows down, loses dexterity and agility, and has to take bigger, longer, more embarrassing gulps. I guess I could survive this way, but it's kind of ridiculous. And who knows what irreparable damage is being caused by my occasional dehydration?

By contrast, my friend walks around with a Stanley cup. You know, the ones that have caused stampedes in places like Target. A big, forty-ounce, inconvenient jug of water. All day. Every day. While I think of water once or twice a day and chug it down like an animal in the occasional desperate moments, she stays tethered to her water jug all day. A sip here. A swig there. And her skin, organs, and hair rejoice.

The valley and all it brings—namely, your reconnection to sonship or daughterhood with God—is like water to the soul and spirit. The spirit, the water, the image of God, and the presence of God, all which we find in the valley, are what we are comprised of and what we need. The valley is the venue where we get more of what we are already made of. And just like the body to water, you can either stay tethered to it and drink often—like that friend of mine—or you can stay away and dehydrate. Dehydration may start out as a headache or fatigue, but continued lack of water can drop your blood sugar dangerously low, cause electrolyte imbalances, heat stroke, kidney failure, and yes, even death. Without adequate hydration, you'll find yourself in an ER needing an IV to recover.

The mountain mindset may be necessary to work by day, but are you anchored to the valley enough to relinquish your titles and lie in the valley by evening?

You're the boss all week, but are you anchored enough to exist as just a son or daughter on the weekend? Can you stop working on the Sabbath?

You've been touring all season and God has given you grace as you've ascended the mountain, but can you step down to him and live from being a daughter or son first?

Better yet, in the middle of your song, your board meeting, and your day's parental duties, could you be so anchored in the valley that, for a second, even there, you are reminded that all this greatness, responsibility, and leading still ends with you safe in God's fatherly arms?

I believe we can.

I believe we must.

We can either carry around and keep refilling that Stanley cup of sonship and daughterhood, frequently going back to the Living Water that is in our familial relationship with God—Christ, the Holy Spirit.

Or we could pay a lot more for an IV of saline in the emergency room to rehydrate from the brink of death.

Don't Be like Maurice

Staying anchored to the valley will prevent relational separation from God and psychological burnout from living too long high on the brutal mountain. Our spiritual well-being and our very survival depend on how we prepare in the valley and maintain closeness to that valley mindset while faced with a climb. I don't care how inspired you feel at the moment. I don't care how many people are itching for your production. I don't care how good you feel about your strategy and momentum. We should never climb without spending adequate time in the valley.

Don't do the climb without doing the time!

In the early 1930s, after a "spiritual awakening" and learning about George Mallory and Andrew Irvine's failed Everest attempt in 1924, Maurice Wilson decided he wanted to climb Mount Everest solo. But not the way a mountaineer should, from the bottom up. The former British soldier, who fought in World War I, hatched an ambitious but simple plan: fly a plane to Tibet, crash-land it near the top, and walk to the summit. Impressive, simple—not incredibly smart, though.

Don't do the climb without doing the time!

It might surprise you to hear that Wilson had zero technical mountaineering or alpine experience. In *The Moth and the Mountain*, a book that told his story, the author submitted that "Wilson had hardly climbed anything more challenging than a flight of stairs."[2]

But at least he knew how to fly a plane, right?

Not really. Wilson also lacked flying experience. He took lessons for just two months before embarking on his mission. And if that weren't enough to make him rethink his adventure, due to a permanent injury sustained in the war, his left arm was largely immobile.

While Wilson garnered the enthusiastic applause of the public, the British government and Air Ministry refused to support him and would not allow him to fly in their airspace. Oh, and he was also denied passage for the trek up Everest. He wasn't technically allowed to be on the mountain.

Driven by his own ambition, a religion-girded ego, and a public that tends to push everyone up a mountain, Wilson went anyway.

When he arrived in Purnea, (British) India, authorities again refused him flying passage over Nepal. Officials impounded his plane and only released it when he falsely promised he would give up his mission and return to Britain. (What kind of spiritual awakening has you lying like this?!)

He finally sold his plane and got as far as Darjeeling, where local authorities were mandated to track his movement. Realizing there was no way to crash-land on the mountain, Wilson revised course to set off for Everest on foot. After laying low for a time, he quietly hired three Sherpas, natives to the mountains of Nepal and the Himalayas, who over the years have genetically adapted to the high altitudes. He left his hotel disguised as a Buddhist monk on March 21, 1934. Almost a month later, his party arrived at the Rongbuk Monastery in Tibet. Wilson left behind the Sherpas and took off to base camp alone.

Six days later, he descended back to the monastery, sick and delirious. (I know, shocker.)

Three weeks later he took off again, this time with the Sherpas to help take him to Camp Three. On May 21, Wilson set off from Camp Three. After two failed attempts, he descended back to Camp Three where the Sherpas strongly advised him to abandon his ambitious plan. Ignoring their sage advice, he took off again on the 31st, asking the Sherpas to wait for him for ten days, the amount of time he anticipated it would take for him to reach the summit and descend to Camp Three. The Sherpas waited three weeks. Wilson never returned. His body and diary were found in 1935 by a British expedition.[3]

His final recorded words: "Off again, gorgeous day."[4]

I'm in no position to judge anyone who desires to climb Mount Everest. Those guys and gals are crazy—maybe the good kind of crazy—but normally they aren't crazy enough to *not* prepare. Wilson was a dreamer—ambitious—who strove to succeed where others predicted failure. His lack of preparation, patience, and respect for sage advice, however, cost him his life. No meal prep, no plan for the thin air, no community for support. Now, would he have made it to the top of Everest with mountaineering and flying experience, full mobility of his extremities, the total support of the Sherpas, and even supplemental oxygen? We can't know for sure, but he would have stood a better chance at enjoying the rest of what was a gorgeous day.

Now, It's Your Turn

If you've already begun the climb, before you go any higher without what you need, stop and come down. Shift your mountain mindset to the valley level.

Get control of your ego—that need to compete and keep up with your social media feed. Challenge and quiet the voices that want to convince you that to rest and revel in the presence of God is to lose time, progress, and position.

After you've shut yourself up a little bit, reengage with how far God has brought you. We often miss His divine providence and strategy while we are in the middle of it. Look back and see how God didn't just take care of you as king, boss, worker, and achiever; He took care of you as His *child*. God speaks in many ways and, from my experience, the protection, provision, and plans that He has established in our lives are sometimes the clearest speakers we can listen to. Hindsight is indeed often twenty-twenty.

Then, as the trip down memory lane inevitably draws your mind both to the beauty and the ugliness of your journey, be reminded that your mountain is a part of a greater terrain, a greater community, and you are *not* the sun everything revolves around. *Call your nephew.* Reengage with the larger family and community around you, and start serving your way down. Go somewhere you can be part of things and not the leader. Serve across to your peers, not down to your subordinates.

Next, engage the tried-and-true method of all the prophets—Moses, Elijah, Elisha, even Jesus himself: Be still and pray. Trust God enough that the industry will be well taken care of as you stop and talk to your Father. And be a son. Be a daughter. Stop doing and spend time being.

Eat in the lush nutrition of the valley before you embark again on the next portion of your mission.

And then, when it's time to climb—either for the first time in your life or for the umpteenth time—plan differently. Don't be surprised by what is up there. You can now prepare for any lack of vegetation or any oxygenless air.

First, take the beauty, the lessons, the identity reminders that you've gained in the valley and pack them up for later. Take note of your weaknesses because the mountain will expose them. Make a playlist. Write some notes to your future climbing self. Schedule in prayer time. Gather your support system. Pack up the valley experience, mindset, and lessons in bite-size portions and carry them with you.

Then, mark your trail. Go up the mountain with more awareness of the moments, the criticisms, the applause, the pressure, and the habits that push you farther up into the cold clouds. And mark those spots! Don't wait for weeks to go by without realizing the triggers that make you unhealthily fixate on your climb. Watch for the moments when you put on your badge, your cape, and your crown so you know what you must take off when the valley calls you back down.

Lastly, don't stay up there for too long. You *will* eventually take on a mountain mindset again. It is necessary for your career, your responsibility, and your assignment. Make sure, however, you never lose your appetite for the valley. Stay anchored to it.

Work on the mountain, but make sure you're doing your living—abundant living—in the valley. Before you go any higher, establish, really establish, your truest identity as a son or daughter of God and see the valley as home.

THE HEADLINER

Man, that mountain mindset certainly has a way of creeping up on you—at the most inappropriate, unnecessary times. It's often just in time to choke the joy, rest, and reward out of a situation and make life, once again, primarily about ascending to new heights or maintaining old ones.

But let me give you a little context.

Right after I turned in this manuscript to the publisher, I set out on another tightly scheduled, thirty-date tour. That is, thirty shows in twenty-eight cities—in about forty days. This one would be a coheadlining ticket with four other dynamic peers in gospel music. And to be honest, I think I handled it well. There are certain stresses that come with touring—just as with any career or calling—that cannot be *valley'd* out. Regardless of the mindset, we must still make sure the buses are maintained, the hotels are booked, and we get to every city on time, whether that means flying, driving, or walking. Every crowd presents its challenges. Sometimes the audience is so excited, they stand and sing louder than we do. And sometimes the chairs are so comfortable, it takes work to keep them awake and engaged. Every venue and its overzealous staff present their own challenges too. Sometimes the dressing rooms are within feet of the stage. Other times I have to walk out of the building and back in, trying to convince security that it is, in fact, my face on the sign and my name on the marquee. Plus, every bandmate is fallible. Sometimes they nail every song and sometimes they feel the pressure. Most of all, every night our performer egos and senses of self are "on the line." That is, if our proverbial loins aren't girded up.

Performing, managing, and pacing yourself while on tour takes some major boss-level confidence and competence every night, but that doesn't mean I can't stay anchored to the valley and the restful sonship it offers. So, before we left on this tour, I prepared.

And I don't just mean rehearsing and arranging the perfect set. Or making sure there were plenty of snacks and Pedialyte in my RV. That's important, for sure, but I mean this *new* kind of meal prep. The type that brings some daily or situational doses of the valley up on the mountain as I work through the week's demands. In between packing a wardrobe and allergy medicine, I also had to pack some reminders.

First, I revised the little "For Depression" note in my phone with up-to-date information. That is, up-to-date *reasons* why I don't need to be down on my life. I made a list of people I could rely on to vent to and potentially be encouraged by. (I've learned that simply making this list keeps the isolating mountain sickness to a minimum.) For a week leading up to the first show, I made a playlist of songs that naturally put me back in a "child's place." They either reminded me of my dependent relationship with God (think "No Longer Slaves" by Bethel) or they reminded me of simpler days (think "This I Promise You" by NSYNC).

I also added reminders of those ego-quieting mantras.

"I can't live off what the mountain gives me." No matter how good or relieving the applause feels, its effect will fade away as quickly as the sun sets daily behind the horizon. So I must pursue more meaningful moments, more permanent words, particularly from a more unconditional source of love.

"I'm important, but not that important." My job is mostly showing up and availing myself to God. Before anything else, I am honored to be used and trusted by God.

And "I only want *God's* idea of success." A successful night for Him may look like one quiet, tough guy in the back, showing no emotion, feeling inspired to follow Jesus. I wouldn't have felt that. There would have been no clear indication in the general applause or lack thereof to let me know that. And that's OK. We do what we do and detach from the results a bit. There's no way we'll ever know the totality of those results anyway.

To top it off, I took the two Power Rangers from my cousin Sydney's Valley Starter Kit and stuck them on a shelf in my tour bus. Just to remind me that, no matter what happened in that theater, I was still a child of God as I finished the night in the RV.

I was proud of myself—still proud—that I prepared *more* for my soul and body to be maintained than I prepared for my performance onstage.

And it worked!

City after city, I resisted the urge to stay on the mountain, to prove myself to people who could care less, or to ignore the folks who were already satisfied with who they knew me to be. I settled into a groove where the day's work didn't bleed into my evenings. Instead of keeping myself up every night, worrying if I was losing ground to my colleagues or somehow regressing in the eyes of the public, I went to sleep.

About halfway through the tour, I packed a small bag to leave the tour and fly to Atlanta. BMI, a very significant organization in the music industry, was honoring me with the Champion Award aimed at celebrating artists in their prime who are making a noteworthy impact on the genre. This was the first time BMI would ever give such an honor to a gospel artist. Up until now, you had to be past your glory years and deep into your legendary status to earn a musical tribute and trophy from them.

I was a first.

I am admittedly not the best at receiving even *regular* honor, though (like a compliment on my outfit). And I barely celebrate *anything*. But whether I was comfortable or not, this event was rolling in. So I did my best not to stress.

I even invited my niece and nephew to be my guests because, well, "*Call your nephew.*"

The day arrived with beautiful weather and plenty of sunshine. My niece and nephew, "the kids," met me in my hotel room, and I let my favorite Gen Z-ers approve my outfit before we headed off to the banquet. We settled into the fun lights of the transport van, mentally preparing ourselves for the hoopla. That is, checking outfits one more time, seeing how much of the layout and vibe we could predict, and finally reminding ourselves that we had no pressure to be anything but ourselves.

After the kids, my photographer, and I jumped out of the Sprinter, I shyly walked toward my first stop: the red carpet. Executives, the genre's top artists, radio personalities, and photographers informally cleared a path through the crowded lobby as my party sauntered toward the chaos. The interviewers sang my praises. Random attendees stopped me to tell me they came because I "deserve this." Once the photographers had taken their pictures of me and the kids and we headed for our seats—as people continued to kiss, hug, smile, shake my hand, and compliment me—I felt a familiar shadow haunt me.

I guess in today's modern psychology book it'd be called "imposter syndrome." But it is this nagging sense that the higher up I go, the more likely I'll be found undeserving of those heights. The success may be clear externally, but not felt internally. Everyone else sees it, validates it, and came to a lavish brunch in Atlanta, in part, to celebrate it. But it's still hard for *me* to see it. And trust it. I made a slow lap around the room, hugging everyone I knew, complimenting countless suits and their wives, but then sat uncomfortably, wondering if I'd have any chance to vanquish the shadow and prove myself worthy.

In a room, an event, convened to celebrate my worth.

See, for a lot of us, the mountain mindset is so chronic—so insidious—because it is our first resort whenever our ego feels uncovered, our résumé is in question, and our value appears to be unsubstantiated. We can feel that way—I felt that way—even when the room is decidedly expressing otherwise.

As they began the beautiful program marked by some of the most talented singers and musicians in the world, my heart pounded and I prayed that somehow, through my actions, or through someone else's, I'd *earn* approval. Even when the climb is noble and God-given, it is often this feeling that not only pushes us farther up into unfriendly air, but also strangles out the joys, the rewards, and the blessings that God gives us.

All tour long I had managed to stay a son, thinking like a son, relaxing in my lane and my labor, free from depression and long bouts of self-doubt and people-pleasing. But now, at what should be a celebration of what has *already been done*, I felt the nagging need to do more. Instead of simply enjoying all the preliminaries, I struggled to *look* like I did. Up until this moment, I didn't want to overthink things and trusted myself to improvise the acceptance speech like I'd always done. But this time, in the eleventh hour, I sat with my Notes app open, wondering if I could write the perfect speech that'd win me favor with the peers, executives, and legends in the room. Again, *that I had already won favor with*!

Not that the banquet food is ever amazing anyway, but I was too nervous to eat. Instead, I sat there with a forced smile and sweaty palms, preoccupied with whether someone else deserved this seat over me.

And then *my part* began. They started to run through my résumé, the accolades, the well-wishes. Even Jazmine Sullivan, R&B superstar, sent in a video to congratulate me.

And then the musical tributes. My goodness. DOE, the artist I first signed to my label. Fantastic. Daryl Walls, one of the greatest singers of our generation and, surprisingly, a distant cousin. Breathtaking. Jason Nelson, just pure greatness. The knot in my stomach squeezed so tightly that surprisingly—to everyone—it broke my face. I teared up as they masterfully presented my catalog and the room joined in the choruses, often with tears on their faces too.

After the last note, they called me up onstage and handed me the microphone. I'm sure Catherine Brewton of BMI hoped for a musical reprise—for me to weave into my own take on the last song and out to a poised, joyful acceptance speech, but, well, I couldn't hold it together! I was verklempt as I unsuccessfully held back tears. I looked down at my phone, through watery eyes, at the speech I had been trying to write and only saw gibberish. I ended up delivering some weird rant that, of course, made me feel quite naked by the time I sat back down in my seat. It was certainly not mountain-level preparation nor presentation. I'd give that speech a D-plus, at best.

But my niece said, "It was really good."

And a fellow artist said, "Now we all understand you a bit more."

Another said, "We can feel your heart."

And another said, "Na-na na-na boo boo. You cried!"

The triumph of the day wasn't professional. I don't think I exuded elite work ethic or poise. Just as my head was climbing back into the clouds, my heart took the stage. Just as the artist hoped to prove his worth, the son proved his.

As I collected myself and the rest of the program zipped by, I started to recount what my heart and I had just blurted out. I remember saying, "All I ever wanted to be was a good man." Earlier that day on the red carpet, a radio personality from Atlanta, Veda Howard, had introduced me as "the man of the hour . . . songwriter, artist . . . *good guy*." I recalled that moment in my speech because while she started with my greatness, the inclusion, the unnecessary and uncommon inclusion, of my apparent and hopefully agreed-upon *goodness* meant way more. The words "good guy" had a similar effect as when, that one time, my dad called me a "good son."

While "great" puts at ease my productive mind and fragile ego, "good" touches something even deeper in my heart. Deeper in my identity. Likely, the part that believes I am a son of God, called to goodness first. That day, God, through His people, through my friends and my community, finally got it through to me that he was proud and that this next season would be about receiving his valley-type love and affirmation more than it'd be about giving another mountain-type offering to the world.

My party and I rushed out of the banquet soon after and started the three-hour drive to Augusta, Georgia, for the next show that night. In my banquet suit, I mounted the stage once again, surer of who I was than ever before.

ACKNOWLEDGMENTS

Special thanks to Mom for giving me almost all my experience as a son and for believing God, my Father, when He told you He'd "handle me." Thanks AJ, Syd, Tate, Brit, that girlfriend, and that random mountaineer I met on the elevator.

NOTES

The Opener
1. Lin Manuel Miranda, *Hamilton: An American Musical*, Atlantic Records, 2015, CD.
2. A. C. Shilton, "You Accomplished Something Great. So Now What?," New York Times, May 28, 2019 https://www.nytimes.com/2019/05/28/smarter-living/you-accomplished-something-great-so-now-what.html.

Chapter 1
1. Jonathan McReynolds, "No Gray," track 3 on *Life Music*, Light Records, 2012.

Chapter 2
1. Bob Evans, "3 Questions with Bob Evans: Mountaineer Dave Roskelley," Fox 13: Salt Lake City, March 1, 2020, https://www.fox13now.com/news/3-questions/3-questions-with-bob-evans-mountaineer-dave-roskelley.
2. "Highest-Living Spider," Guinness World Records Limited 2024, accessed February 16, 2024, https://www.guinnessworldrecords.com/world-records/405008-highest-living-spider.
3. Aylin Woodward, Ashley Collman, and Maiya Focht, "What Happens to Your Body in Mount Everest's 'Death Zone,'" *Business Insider*, September 5, https://www.businessinsider.com/mount-everest-death-zone-what-happens-to-body-2019-5.

4. Jamie Shultz, "Friedrich Nietzsche: Morality and Truth," *Fairmont State University Library News Blog*, February 15, 2023, accessed December 17, 2023, https://library.fairmontstate.edu/news/1/Friedrich-Nietzsche-Morality-and-Truth.

5. Christi Carras, "Geoffrey Owens Turns the Tables on Trader Joe's Job Shaming with New Show," *Los Angeles Times*, September 8, 2020, accessed September 21, 2023, https://www.latimes.com/entertainment-arts/tv/story/2020-09-08/geoffrey-owens-cosby-show-actor-trader-joes-instagram.

Chapter 3

1. Adam Roy, "What Are the Most Dangerous National Parks? One Story Got It Wrong," Backpacker, updated September 24, 2023, https://www.backpacker.com/survival/the-10-most-dangerous-national-parks-in-america/.

2. "The World's 15 Most Dangerous Mountains to Climb (by Fatality Rate)," Ultimate Kilimanjaro, accessed February 24, 2024, https://www.ultimatekilimanjaro.com/the-worlds-most-dangerous-mountains/.

3. Acts 9:1–31.

Chapter 4

1. Robert J. Samuelson, "Don't Deny the Link Between Poverty and Single Parenthood," *Washington Post*, March 18, 2018, https://www.washingtonpost.com/opinions/dont-deny-the-link-between-poverty-and-single-parenthood/2018/03/18/e6b0121a-2942-11e8-b79d-f3d931db7f68_story.html.

Chapter 5

1. Rev. Milton Brunson & the Thompson Community Singers, "Great Things," from *If I Be Lifted*, 1987, posted July 31, 2020, by Gospel Nostalgia, YouTube, https://www.youtube.com/watch?v=OAPIbZd7gW4.

2. Jonathan McReynolds, "People," track 2 on *People*, Entertainment One US, 2020.

3. Cory N., reply to "Coping with Exposure," Mountain Project, December 1, 2023, accessed February 6, 2024, https://www

.mountainproject.com/forum/topic/125427337/coping-with
-exposure.

4. Tam McTavish, reply to "Why Is Climbing Down Scarier Than
Climbing Up?," Quora, 2017, accessed February 6, 2024,
https://www.quora.com/Why-is-climbing-down-scarier-than
-climbing-up.

5. Tyler Taggart, reply to "Why Is Climbing Down Scarier Than
Climbing Up?"

Chapter 6

1. "Acclimatization," Mountain Professor, accessed April 3, 2024,
https://www.mountainprofessor.com/acclimatization.html.

2. Aylin Woodward, "Crowds, Costs, and Corpses: 16
Misconceptions About What It's Like to Climb Everest," *Business
Insider*, May 30, 2019, https://www.businessinsider.com/mount
-everest-misconceptions-about-climbing-2019-5.

3. Trent Toone, "There and Back Again: Mormons on Mount
Everest," Deseret News, June 10, 2013, https://www.deseret
.com/2013/6/10/20521053/there-and-back-again-mormons-on
-mount-everest/.

4. Stacy Jo Dixon, "Number of Social Media Users Worldwide
from 2017 to 2028," Statista, May 17, 2024, https://www.statista
.com/statistics/278414/number-of-worldwide-social-network
-users/.

Chapter 7

1. Tye Tribbett, sermon, Live Church Orlando, Orlando, FL, 2024.

Chapter 8

1. "Food on Everest: What to Eat and How It Gets to the
Mountain," Alpenglow Expeditions, accessed May 21, 2024,
https://alpenglowexpeditions.com/blog/food-on-everest-what
-to-eat-and-how-it-gets-to-the-mountain#:~:text=The%20
team%20snacks%20a%20lot,can%20to%20combat%20big
%20days.

2. Jonathan Dunn, "Perfect Peace," track 1 on *Keep My Mind*,
Jonathan Dunn, 2015.

NOTES

Chapter 9

1. Barry M. Popkin, Kristen E. D'Anci, and Irwin H. Rosenberg, "Water, Hydration and Health," *Nutrition Reviews* 68, no. 8 (2010): 439–458, https://www.ncbi.nlm.nih.gov/pmc/articles /PMC2908954/.
2. Ed Caesar, *The Moth and the Mountain: A True Story of Love, War, and Everest* (Avid Reader Press, 2020), Kindle edition.
3. T. S. Blakeney, "Maurice Wilson and Everest, 1934," *The Alpine Journal* (1965), 269, https://www.alpinejournal.org.uk/Contents /Contents_1965_files/AJ%201965%20269-274%20Blakeney% 20Maurice%20Wilson.pdf.
4. Caesar, *The Moth and the Mountain*, 214, Kindle edition.

ABOUT THE AUTHOR

Jonathan McReynolds is a Grammy Award–winning artist, songwriter, and producer known for his creative and strikingly honest approach to music. Over the past decade, he has released five acclaimed albums and authored two books, while also serving as an adjunct professor at Columbia College Chicago. His talents extend to the screen, where he has appeared in various TV series and films, including the highly rated television series *Sunday Best*. Jonathan's work often reflects his belief in the importance of "making room" for God amid the chaos and busyness of modern life. He holds a bachelor of music from Columbia College and a master of arts in biblical studies from Moody Theological Seminary.